The Herbal Remedies Handbook for Beginners

A Complete Guide to Natural Healing with 100+ Effective Recipes Using Common Herbs for Everyday Health

by

Eva Greenleaf

eBook ISBN: 978-1-917358-11-8

Paperback ISBN: 978-1-917358-12-5

Hardcover ISBN: 978-1-917358-13-2

About the Author

"Can nature truly heal?" This question has fueled my passion for over 20 years. I'm Eva Greenleaf, and my journey into the world of herbalism has been one of discovery and transformation.

With a wealth of knowledge in herbal medicine, including Ayurvedic, traditional Chinese, and Western practices, I've witnessed the profound impact of natural remedies on countless lives. My mission is to demystify these age-old traditions, making them accessible and practical for everyone.

I live immersed in nature, cultivating a vibrant herb garden where I continually explore new remedies. My dedication to environmental sustainability and ethical sourcing ensures that my practices are as kind to the earth as they are effective.

Why am I writing this book? Because I believe in the power of herbs to heal and empower. This book is a labor of love, designed to equip you with practical advice and effective recipes to create your own natural remedies. My hope is that it will inspire and guide you on your own herbal journey.

Warm regards,

Eva Greenleaf

Table of Contents

Introduction

Imagine a world where your kitchen holds the secrets to enhanced health and well-being—where each herb and spice in your pantry serves not just to enhance flavor, but to fortify your body against ailments. What if I told you that the path to this enriched life is right at your fingertips, and it starts with the humblest of garden plants?

This guide unveils the potent world of herbal remedies, a tradition as old as time but as new as each leaf that unfurls in the spring. Here, we rediscover the forgotten wisdom of our ancestors, who used the earth's bounty to heal, soothe, and nourish. This book is more than just a compendium of herbal recipes; it is a doorway to a more attuned way of living, one that aligns with the natural rhythms of the earth and our bodies.

A Journey Through Time and Nature

You will embark on a historical voyage, tracing the green threads that connect the ancient past to our modern lives. Learn how civilizations from the Egyptians to the Chinese have used botanicals not only to heal but to forge connections with nature. The narrative then brings you to the present, exploring how these enduring practices can be integrated into contemporary health routines.

Harnessing the Power of Herbs for Health

As we delve deeper into the benefits of herbal medicine, you'll discover how these plants do more than treat illness—they enhance life. You'll learn about the ecological gifts of herbs that support life on our planet by promoting biodiversity and sustainable practices. This book offers practical insights into how you can harness these benefits, transforming the theoretical into the tangible.

Practical Applications for Everyday Health

Detailed profiles of over 100 herbs will guide you through their uses, helping you understand how to apply their healing properties in your life. From soothing teas to healing salves, each recipe is designed to offer relief and enhancement for a variety of ailments, ensuring that you have the tools to care for your health naturally.

Creating Your Herbal Apothecary

Practical advice on setting up your own home apothecary ensures that you're prepared to embark on your herbal journey. Safety tips, dosage guidelines, and methods of herb preparation will equip you with the knowledge to use herbs effectively and safely.

For Everyone Who Seeks a Natural Path to Health

Whether you are taking your first steps into herbal remedies or are a seasoned practitioner looking to expand your knowledge, this book offers a comprehensive overview that appeals to all levels of experience. It invites you to explore, to learn, and to grow along with your herbal garden.

So, are you ready to embark on a transformative journey with herbs? Let this handbook be your guide and companion as you unlock the powerful secrets of natural healing, one herb at a time. Rediscover the joy and simplicity of living in tune with nature. The path to natural health begins here, and it promises to be as enriching as it is enlightening.

Let's begin this beautiful journey together.

Part I
The History

Chapter 1
From Ancient Roots to Modern Uses

Herbology is a practice that has evolved from ancient roots to modern uses. This chapter will guide you through the history of herbal practices, from the earliest civilizations to contemporary times, showing how the wisdom of the past continues to influence and enrich our lives today.

Ancient Herbal Practices

The use of herbal remedies has been around for centuries. The knowledge of medicinal plants was passed down through generations and civilizations. These ancient practices not only provided the basis for modern herbalism but also demonstrated the profound understanding that early cultures had of the natural world and its potential to heal. Exploring these traditions offers valuable insights into the evolution and enduring relevance of herbal medicine.

Herbal medicine is a practice as old as civilization itself, with roots extending deep into ancient societies. The Egyptians, for example, were known for their extensive use of medicinal plants. They documented their knowledge in texts such as the Ebers Papyrus, a medical document from around 1550 BCE that lists hundreds of herbal remedies. The Egyptians utilized plants like aloe vera for healing wounds and infections and garlic for its cardiovascular benefits.

In China, Ancient Chinese texts such as the "Shennong Bencao Jing" (Divine Farmer's Materia Medica) from around 200-300 CE detail the use of numerous herbs. Ginseng, for instance, was revered for its energy-boosting and immune-strengthening properties, while ginger was commonly used to treat digestive issues.

India's Ayurvedic tradition, dating back over 3,000 years, is another cornerstone of ancient herbal practice. Ayurveda focuses on balancing the body's three doshas (Vata, Pitta, and Kapha) through diet, lifestyle, and herbal treatments. Herbs like turmeric, with its anti-inflammatory properties, and ashwagandha, known for its stress-relieving effects, are staples in Ayurvedic medicine (Petrovska, 2012).

The Greeks and Romans also made significant contributions to herbal medicine. The Greek physician Hippocrates, often called the "Father of Medicine," advocated for the use of herbs as part of a holistic approach to health. Later, Dioscorides, a Greek physician in the Roman army, compiled "De Materia Medica," a comprehensive herbal manual that was used for centuries. The Romans, influenced by Greek practices, adopted and expanded upon this knowledge, using herbs like fennel for digestion and rosemary for memory enhancement (Phair, 2021).

Medieval and Renaissance Herbology

During the Medieval and Renaissance periods, the practice of herbology experienced significant growth and transformation in Europe. In the Middle Ages, monasteries became centers of herbal knowledge, where monks cultivated medicinal plants in their gardens and transcribed ancient texts.

The Renaissance brought a renewed interest in classical knowledge, including the herbal traditions of ancient Greece and Rome. This period saw the publication of numerous herbals, and comprehensive books detailing the properties and uses of plants.

The printing press, invented in the 15th century, played a crucial role in providing herbal knowledge more widely than ever before. The combination of revived classical wisdom and new scientific inquiries during the Renaissance significantly enriched the field of herbology, bridging the gap between ancient practices and contemporary herbal medicine (Team, 2023).

European Herbalism

During the Medieval period in Europe, herbal knowledge was preserved and expanded upon by monastic communities. Monks in monasteries cultivated medicinal gardens and copied ancient texts, ensuring the survival of herbal wisdom through turbulent times. One notable text from this era is the "Physica" by Hildegard of Bingen, a 12th-century abbess who wrote extensively about the healing properties of plants (Pieroni, 2013).

The Renaissance marked a revival of learning and interest in natural sciences, including herbal medicine. Herbalists such as Paracelsus challenged traditional medical practices and emphasized the importance of observation and experimentation. The publication of herbals, and detailed books about plants and their medicinal uses, flourished during this period. One famous example is "Herball, or Generall Historie of Plantes" by John Gerard, published in 1597, which became a standard reference for herbalists.

Colonial and Native American Herbal Practices

In the Colonial period, European settlers in the Americas encountered a rich tradition of Native American herbal medicine. Native American tribes had a deep understanding of the local flora and its medicinal properties, often gained through centuries of observation and use (Boye, 2024). Plants like echinacea for immune support and willow bark, a natural source of salicylic acid (the basis for aspirin), were commonly used by Native Americans (Mortlock, 2022).

European settlers quickly learned from Native American herbal knowledge and integrated it with their own practices. This exchange of knowledge led to a unique blend of European and indigenous herbal traditions. The colonists adopted local plants and remedies, which were then recorded in new herbal texts, contributing to the broader body of herbal knowledge.

Modern Herbal Medicine

Modern herbal medicine combines ancient traditions with scientific research, creating a bridge between historical wisdom and modern medical practices. Over the past century, advancements in botanical pharmacology have deepened our understanding of how plant compounds interact with the human body. This scientific exploration has led to the discovery and validation of numerous active ingredients in herbs, many of which have found their place in conventional medicine.

The 20th and 21st centuries have witnessed an increase of interest in herbal medicine. This renewed interest is driven by a preference for natural health solutions and concerns about the potential side effects of synthetic drugs. Additionally, there is a growing awareness of the importance of sustainable healthcare practices. Today, herbal supplements and remedies are widely embraced, backed by both traditional knowledge and scientific validation.

Current trends in herbal medicine show the importance of quality control and standardization of herbal products. Organizations such as the World Health Organization (WHO) and the National Center for Complementary and Integrative Health (NCCIH) are crucial in promoting and regulating herbal medicine on a global scale. As the field of modern herbal medicine evolves, it offers a complementary approach to health and wellness that honors its historical origins while incorporating contemporary scientific advancements.

Developments in Botanical Pharmacology

The 19th and 20th centuries saw significant advancements in botanical pharmacology, the scientific study of medicinal plants. Researchers began isolating active compounds from plants, leading to the development of many modern drugs. For instance, the discovery of quinine from cinchona bark provided a powerful treatment for malaria, and the isolation of morphine from opium poppies revolutionized pain management (Asim Najmi, 2022).

Advancements in analytical techniques, such as chromatography and mass spectrometry, have enabled scientists to identify and quantify the active constituents in medicinal plants. This scientific approach has validated many traditional uses of herbs and uncovered new therapeutic applications.

Current Trends

Today, herbal medicine is experiencing a resurgence in popularity as people seek natural and holistic approaches to health. There is a growing interest in integrating herbal remedies with conventional medicine, leading to the development of integrative medicine practices that combine the best of both worlds. Herbal supplements and products are widely available, and many people use them for preventive health, wellness, and treating minor ailments.

Current trends in herbal medicine also include a focus on sustainability and ethical sourcing. Consumers and practitioners are increasingly aware of the environmental impact of harvesting wild plants and the importance of preserving biodiversity. This has led to a rise in the cultivation of medicinal herbs and the use of organic and locally sourced ingredients.

Herbal medicine has seen the evolution from traditional to modern scientific approaches. Does not matter if you are a beginner or an experienced practitioner, understanding the rich history and current trends in herbal medicine can enhance your appreciation of this timeless healing art and guide you in using herbs effectively for your health and well-being.

Part II
The Benefits

Chapter 2
The Wonders of Herbal Healing

In the world of natural remedies, herbal healing shines as a long-standing practice valued by cultures across generations. The wonders of herbal healing include a broad range of plants and botanicals, each with unique properties contributing to their therapeutic effects.

Understanding the marvels of herbal healing starts with appreciating the plants themselves. Herbs aren't just random greenery; they're rich sources of bioactive compounds that interact with the human body in profound ways. Whether soothing inflammation, boosting immunity, or easing stress, herbs offer a plethora of benefits that complement and enhance our natural healing processes (Deering, 2019).

Exploring herbal healing opens doors to a world of possibilities for maintaining health and vitality. From simple herbal teas to potent tinctures and salves, there are countless ways to tap into the healing power of plants. By learning about the properties and uses of different herbs, individuals can customize their herbal remedies to suit their specific needs and preferences.

Understanding How Herbs Work

Herbs are like nature's medicine cabinet, filled with various components that contribute to their healing properties. Understanding these components can assist you in selecting the appropriate herbs for your needs.

Herbs contain a variety of compounds such as alkaloids, flavonoids, tannins, terpenoids, saponins, and glycosides. Each of these compounds serves different purposes, ranging from pain relief to antimicrobial effects or calming properties (Hoshaw, 2021).

Alkaloids, for instance, have analgesic properties and can enhance alertness. Flavonoids, commonly found in fruits and vegetables, possess antioxidant properties that protect the body from oxidative stress. Tannins have astringent properties and can reduce inflammation. Terpenoids, found in plants like ginkgo and ginseng, exhibit diverse therapeutic effects, including antimicrobial and analgesic properties. (Hoshaw, 2021).

Saponins act as natural detergents and have immune-boosting properties, while glycosides, such as those found in foxglove, have cardiac effects, benefiting heart health.

Understanding these components enables you to choose herbs tailored to your specific needs. For example, if you're experiencing anxiety, herbs containing flavonoids and terpenoids, like chamomile, may help calm your nerves. (Hoshaw, 2021).

Different Ways to Use Herbs

Herbs can be utilized in various forms, including teas, capsules, or creams, each offering distinct benefits.

Teas are prepared by steeping herbs in hot water, allowing the extraction of beneficial compounds. They are suitable for addressing issues such as digestive discomfort or respiratory ailments.

Tinctures involve soaking herbs in alcohol to extract their active constituents, resulting in potent herbal extracts. Tinctures are often used for immune support or managing chronic conditions.

Capsules provide a convenient method of herbal consumption, ideal for individuals who dislike the taste of herbs yet seek their therapeutic benefits.

Creams or ointments are applied topically to the skin and are effective for addressing skin conditions or localized pain relief.

How Herbs Can Help You

Herbs offer a natural approach to addressing various health concerns, providing relief for conditions ranging from digestive discomfort to stress and respiratory issues (Hoshaw, 2021).

For example, ginger and peppermint are effective in alleviating digestive issues such as nausea or bloating.

Herbs like ashwagandha or rhodiola can help reduce stress and increase energy levels.

Eucalyptus or thyme are beneficial for respiratory conditions, offering relief from coughs or congestion.

Certain herbs, such as hawthorn or garlic, support heart health by promoting cardiovascular function and lowering blood pressure.

Echinacea and elderberry are renowned for immune-boosting properties, helping to prevent infections and enhance overall immunity.

With the right selection of herbs, you can address a wide range of health concerns naturally, without relying solely on conventional medications.

.

Chapter 3
Herbs and Their Ecological Gifts

As you understood the history in the first part, and the medicinal benefits of herbs in the previous chapter, it is time to explore the profound ecological advantages that herbs offer. From encouraging biodiversity to aiding in pest control and soil health, herbs are crucial for maintaining the delicate balance of ecosystems.

Ecosystem Biodiversity

Herbs attract a diverse range of pollinators, such as bees, butterflies, and birds, with their vibrant flowers and nectar. These pollinators play a vital role in the reproduction of plants, thereby contributing to the overall health and resilience of the ecosystem.

Additionally, herbs often form the base of complex food webs, serving as a source of nourishment for herbivores and omnivores. By supporting a diverse array of plant and animal life, herbs help maintain the stability and resilience of ecosystems.

Firstly, herbs attract a wide range of pollinators, including bees, butterflies, and birds, with their colorful flowers and sweet nectar. By attracting pollinators, herbs facilitate the fertilization of flowers and the production of seeds, contributing to the propagation and genetic diversity of plant populations (Vidyashree S, .2022).

Moreover, herbs serve as important food sources for a variety of herbivores. The leaves, stems, flowers, and seeds of herbs provide nourishment for these animals, supporting their growth, reproduction, and survival. In turn, herbivores play a crucial role in shaping plant communities by regulating herbivory and influencing plant distribution and abundance.

Additionally, herbs create microhabitats and ecological niches that support a diverse range of organisms. Their dense foliage, intricate branching patterns, and root systems create sheltered spaces and hiding spots for insects, spiders, and other invertebrates. These microhabitats provide refuge from predators, harsh weather conditions, and disturbances, allowing small animals to thrive in their midst. Furthermore, herbs contribute to the structural complexity of ecosystems, adding vertical layers and spatial heterogeneity that increase habitat diversity and species richness (Uwe Schippmann, n.d.).

Furthermore, herbs interact with other plant species and form complex ecological networks that enhance ecosystem resilience and stability. Through allelopathy, the release of chemicals that inhibit the growth of neighboring plants, and herbs influences the distribution and abundance of other species, creating spatial patterns and vegetation zones within ecosystems (Rômulo RN Alves, 2007). These interactions foster dynamic ecological processes, such as succession, colonization, and regeneration, that drive ecosystem dynamics and change over time.

Natural Pest Control

One of the remarkable ecological benefits of herbs is their ability to assist in natural pest control. Many herbs produce compounds that repel or deter pests, thereby reducing the need for harmful chemical pesticides.

For example, herbs like basil, rosemary, and mint emit strong fragrances that act as natural insect repellents. These scents can confuse insects, making it difficult for them to locate their host plants or disrupting their feeding and mating behaviors (WANDLING, 2020). By planting these herbs alongside susceptible crops or in garden beds, farmers and gardeners can create a protective barrier that deters pests and reduces crop damage.

In addition to repelling pests, some herbs attract beneficial insects that act as natural predators or parasites of pest species. These beneficial insects help regulate pest populations by feeding on or parasitizing pest insects, thereby reducing their numbers and preventing outbreaks (WANDLING, 2020). By providing habitat and food sources for these beneficial predators, herbs contribute to a more balanced and sustainable ecosystem.

For instance, herbs like dill, fennel, and yarrow attract predatory insects such as ladybugs, lacewings, and parasitic wasps. These insects feed on aphids, caterpillars, and other common garden pests, helping to keep their populations in check. By interplanting these herbs with susceptible crops or establishing insectary plants in garden borders, farmers and gardeners can attract and retain beneficial insects, creating a natural buffer against pest infestations (Critchley, 2019).

Furthermore, some herbs possess allelopathic properties, meaning they release chemicals that inhibit the growth or development of competing plants and pests. For example, herbs like thyme, oregano, and marigold produce allelochemicals that suppress weed germination and root growth, reducing competition for resources and minimizing weed pressure in garden beds.

Soil Enrichment and Erosion Prevention

Herbs play a crucial role in enriching soil health and preventing erosion, thereby safeguarding the integrity of terrestrial ecosystems. Through their root systems and organic matter, herbs help improve soil structure, fertility, and moisture retention.

Herbs contribute organic matter to the soil through the decomposition of their leaves, stems, and roots. This organic matter serves as a nutrient source for soil microorganisms and promotes the formation of humus, that improves fertility of soil over time (Roundy, 2023).

Furthermore, herbs with dense foliage provide ground cover, reducing soil erosion caused by wind and water. By anchoring soil particles and reducing surface runoff, these herbs help prevent the loss of valuable topsoil and protect against land degradation.

Part III
THE HERBAL REMEDIES

Chapter 4
Introduction to Herbal Remedies

Rooted in ancient traditions and passed down through generations, herbal remedies harness the therapeutic properties of plants to address several health concerns. Recently, the interest in herbal medicine has increased because people seek safer, more sustainable alternatives to synthetic drugs.

Understanding the basic principles of herbal remedies is essential for anyone interested in exploring natural healing modalities. This introductory chapter serves as a primer on herbal medicine, providing an overview of its history, principles, and practical applications.

Understanding Common Ailments

To effectively utilize herbal remedies, it is crucial to grasp the nature of common ailments that they can address. These ailments encompass a broad spectrum of health issues ranging from mild discomforts to chronic conditions. Digestive disturbances like indigestion, bloating, and constipation, respiratory problems such as coughs, colds, and asthma, skin disorders like acne, eczema, and rashes, and stress-related ailments including anxiety, insomnia, and headaches are just a few examples.

Each ailment manifests with distinct symptoms and underlying causes, and understanding these factors is essential for selecting appropriate herbal treatments. For instance, digestive issues may stem from poor dietary choices, while respiratory problems could result from environmental factors like pollution or allergens. By recognizing the root causes and symptoms of common ailments, individuals can tailor their herbal remedies to address specific needs effectively.

The Role of Herbs in Natural Healing

Herbs have played a significant role in natural healing practices across cultures and civilizations for centuries. Unlike synthetic medications, which often target specific symptoms or conditions, herbs offer a holistic approach to health and wellness.

One of the key advantages of herbal remedies is their gentle yet potent nature. Rather than masking symptoms, herbs address the underlying imbalances or dysfunctions within the body, supporting its innate ability to heal itself. For example, herbs like ginger and peppermint can soothe digestive discomfort by reducing inflammation and promoting healthy digestion, while chamomile and lavender can calm the nervous system and alleviate stress-related symptoms (Chaughule, 2023).

Overview of 100 Herbs for Common Ailments

Aloe Vera

Origin: It was originated in North Africa but is now cultivated worldwide, especially in regions with a warm climate.

Aloe vera can be grown indoors or outdoors in well-draining soil and requires ample sunlight.

Aloe vera plants can be found in nurseries, garden centers, or online.

Application: Aloe vera gel is used to soothe burns, cuts, and skin irritations.

Amalaki (Amla)

Origin: Amalaki, also known as Indian Gooseberry, originates from India and Southeast Asia.

Amalaki trees require a warm climate and well-draining soil. They can be grown from seeds or cuttings.

Fresh or dried Amalaki fruits can be found in specialty grocery stores or online.

Application: Amalaki fruits can be consumed fresh, dried, or in powdered form. They are known for boosting immunity and aiding digestion.

Anise

Origin: Anise was firstly found in the Eastern Mediterranean region and Southwest Asia.

The plants thrive in dry soil and full sunlight. They grow from seeds directly sown into the ground or in pots.

Anise seeds are available in spice shops, supermarkets, and online.

Application: Anise seeds are common spice and can also be used to make herbal tea or infused in hot water to aid digestion and relieve cough.

Ashwagandha

Origin: Ashwagandha, also known as Indian ginseng, originates from India, the Middle East, and parts of Africa.

Ashwagandha plants prefer dry and sandy soil with plenty of sunlight. They can be grown from seeds or propagated from cuttings.

Ashwagandha supplements are available in health food stores, herbal shops, and online.

Application: Ashwagandha roots are dried and ground into a powder, which can be used in any form, tea, tinctures, or capsules. It is known for its adaptogenic properties. It helps in managing stress and anxiety. Also., it boosts energy.

Astragalus

Origin: Astragalus is native to China and Mongolia but is now grown in various regions worldwide.

Astragalus roots and supplements are available in health food stores, herbal shops, and online.

Application: Astragalus roots are dried and used to make herbal tea or taken in capsule form. It is known for its immune-boosting properties and ability to combat fatigue.

Basil

Origin: Basil originated in Central Africa and Southeast Asia.

Basil thrives in warm climates and prefers well-drained soil with plenty of sunlight. Plant the seeds or cuttings in moist soil, spacing them about 12 inches apart. Water regularly and trim the leaves to encourage bushier growth.

Basil can be found in nurseries, garden centers, or even supermarkets in the fresh produce section. Seeds or seedlings are also available at gardening stores or online.

Application: Basil leaves are commonly used fresh in cooking, adding flavor to salads, pasta dishes, soups, and sauces. It can also be used to make pesto or infused into oils and kinds of vinegar.

Medicinally, basil is known for its digestive properties and can be brewed into tea to soothe upset stomachs or alleviate headaches.

Bay Leaf

Origin: Bay leaf, also known as laurel leaf, originates from the Mediterranean region, where it has been used in cooking and medicine for thousands of years.

Bay leaf trees can be grown in containers or directly in the ground in warm climates. Bay trees are slow-growing and can be propagated from cuttings or purchased as young plants.

Fresh or dried bay leaves can be found in the spice section of grocery stores. Bay leaf trees can be purchased from nurseries or online plant retailers.

Application: Bay leaves are commonly used whole or ground in cooking to add flavor to soups, stews, sauces, and marinades. They should be removed before serving as they can be tough and indigestible. Bay leaves are also used in herbal remedies for respiratory issues and digestive ailments when brewed into tea or infused into oil.

Black Cohosh

Origin: Black cohosh is native to eastern North America, where it has been traditionally used by Native American tribes for its medicinal properties.

Black cohosh prefers moist, woodland environments and require some shade too. You can sow the seeds or purchase a young plants. Plant in fertile, well-drained soil and keep consistently moist. It takes a few years for black cohosh plants to mature and produce flowers.

Application: Black cohosh is primarily used to relieve symptoms associated with menopause and PMS. It can be taken as a supplement in capsule or tablet form or brewed into a tea. Consult a healthcare professional before using black cohosh, especially if pregnant, breastfeeding, or taking medications.

Black Pepper

Origin: Black pepper is native to India and has been used in cooking and medicine for thousands of years. It is used as a common spice all over the world.

Black pepper vines are tropical plants that require a hot and humid climate. They can be grown in containers or trained to climb up trellises or trees. Plant in well-drained soil with plenty of organic matter and provide support for the vines to climb. Black pepper is readily available in supermarkets, spice shops, and online retailers. It can be purchased whole or ground.

Application: Black pepper is used to add flavor and heat to a wide variety of dishes. It can be used whole, cracked, or ground. Medicinally, black pepper aids digestion, stimulates appetite, and promotes respiratory health. It can be brewed into a tea or incorporated into herbal remedies for colds and coughs.

Black Seed (Nigella)

Origin: Black seed, also known as Nigella sativa, originated in southwestern Asia. It is a traditional medicine for centuries.

Black seed plants are annual flowering herbs that thrive in warm, sunny climates, in dry soil.

Black seed oil and supplements are available in health food stores, pharmacies, and online retailers. The seeds themselves can also be found in some specialty food stores or online.

Application: Black seed has anti-inflammatory properties and can reduce symptoms of asthma and other respiratory conditions. It can be consumed as an oil, added to food or beverages, or taken in supplement form. Consult a healthcare professional before using black seed, especially if pregnant, breastfeeding, or taking medications.

Borage

Origin: Borage, also known as Borago officinalis, is native to the Mediterranean region and has been renowned for it culinary and medicinal uses since ancient times.

Borage seeds, seedlings, and dried leaves are available in some garden centers, nurseries, and online retailers. Fresh leaves and flowers can also be found in some specialty food stores or farmers' markets.

Application: Borage is an annual herb that prefers dry soil. Plant the seeds into the ground in the spring after the last frost, or start seeds indoors and transplant seedlings once the weather warms up. Borage plants self-seed readily and can become invasive if not controlled.

Borage is beneficial for skin health and reducing inflammation. The leaves and flowers can be eaten raw in salads or used as a garnish. You can also make tea or infuse them into oil for topical use. Borage supplements are available in capsule or oil form. Use them orally to promote skin health and reduce inflammation.

Burdock Root

Origin: Burdock, also known as Arctium lappa, originated in Europe and Asia and has been used in traditional Chinese and Ayurvedic medicine for centuries.

Application: Burdock is a biennial plant that prefers moist soil and partial shade. Plant directly into the ground in the spring or fall, as burdock plants require a cold period to germinate.

Burdock root supplements, tinctures, and dried root slices are available in health food stores, pharmacies, and online retailers. Fresh burdock root can sometimes be found in specialty grocery stores or farmers' markets.

Burdock root supports detoxification processes and helps with skin issues. It can be consumed fresh, cooked, or dried and brewed into a tea. Use capsules for detoxification.

Calendula

Origin: Calendula, also known as Calendula officinalis, is native to the Mediterranean region and has been used in traditional medicine for centuries.

Application: Calendula is effective in healing wounds and treating various skin conditions. The flowers can be infused into oil or made into a salve or cream for topical use. Calendula extracts can also be taken orally to promote skin healing and reduce inflammation.

Calendula flowers, leaves, and extracts are available in health food stores, pharmacies, and online retailers. Fresh calendula flowers can sometimes be found in specialty food stores or farmers' markets.

Camphor

Origin: Camphor is derived from the wood of the camphor tree, native to East Asia, particularly China and Japan. It has been used in traditional medicine for its therapeutic properties.

Application: Camphor provides pain relief and helps with congestion when applied topically or inhaled. It can be used as an ingredient in creams, ointments, and balms for muscle aches and pains. When added to hot water or a vaporizer, camphor oil can help relieve congestion and respiratory symptoms. Camphor oil, creams, and ointments are available in health food stores, pharmacies, and online retailers. Pure camphor crystals can also be purchased for use in DIY remedies and aromatherapy.

Cardamom

Origin: Cardamom is a spice native to the Indian subcontinent and Southeast Asia. It has a warm, slightly sweet flavor and is commonly used in both sweet and savory dishes.

Application: Cardamom aids digestion and freshens breath. It can be used in cooking, baking, or brewing as a tea. Add ground cardamom to desserts, curries, and rice dishes. For a refreshing breath freshener, you can chew on whole cardamom pods after meals.

Catnip

Origin: Catnip, scientifically known as Nepeta cataria, is a herbaceous plant belonging to the mint family. It is native to Europe and Asia but has been naturalized in North America.

Application: Catnip helps with insomnia and anxiety. It can be brewed into a soothing tea or used in aromatherapy to promote relaxation. To make catnip tea, steep dried catnip leaves in hot water for 5-10 minutes, then strain and enjoy before bedtime to aid sleep or during times of stress to help reduce anxiety.

Cayenne Pepper

Origin: Cayenne pepper is a hot chili pepper commonly used to add spice and flavor to dishes. It is native to Central and South America but is now cultivated worldwide.

Application: Cayenne pepper improves circulation and provides pain relief. It can be added to savory dishes, soups, and sauces to add heat and depth of flavor. Cayenne pepper can also be used topically as a natural pain reliever for sore muscles and joints. To make a topical paste, mix ground cayenne pepper with a small amount of olive oil and apply to the affected area.

Chamomile

Origin: Chamomile, derived from the Matricaria chamomilla plant, is a flowering herb native to Europe and Western Asia. It has a mild, floral flavor and is commonly consumed as a tea for its calming effects.

Application: Chamomile reduces anxiety. Use chamomile tea before bed to promote relaxation and improve sleep quality. Chamomile also has a use in aromatherapy and promotes relaxation by reducing stress.

Chasteberry (Vitex)

Origin: Chasteberry is native to the Mediterranean region. It has hormone-balancing properties.

Application: Chasteberry helps maintain hormonal balance and alleviates PMS symptoms. It can be taken as a supplement in capsule or tincture form. Chasteberry supplements are commonly used by women to regulate menstrual cycles and reduce bloating and mood swings. It important to consult with a healthcare professional before using chasteberry, especially if you are pregnant, breastfeeding, or taking hormone medications.

Cinnamon

Origin: Cinnamon is derived from the inner bark of trees belonging to the Cinnamomum genus, native to Southeast Asia. It has a sweet, warm flavor and is commonly used as a spice in both sweet and savory dishes.

Application: Cinnamon regulates blood sugar levels and aids digestion. It can be added to baked goods, oatmeal, smoothies, and hot beverages such as tea and coffee. Ground cinnamon can also be sprinkled on fruit, yogurt, and toast for added flavor and health benefits.

Clove

Origin: Clove is derived from the flower buds of the Syzygium aromaticum tree, native to Indonesia. It has a strong, spicy flavor and is commonly used as a spice in cooking and baking.

Application: Clove provides relief for toothaches and aids digestion. It can be used whole or ground in savory dishes, stews, and desserts. Clove oil gives temporary relief of toothache pain.

Additionally, clove oil can be diluted with carrier oil and massaged onto the abdomen to relieve digestive discomfort.

Comfrey

Origin: Comfrey is a perennial herb originated from Europe and Asia. It has large, hairy leaves and produces clusters of purple, pink, or white flowers.

Application: Comfrey is effective in healing wounds and reducing inflammation. It can be applied topically as a poultice or ointment to promote wound healing, reduce swelling, and relieve pain. Comfrey can also be brewed into tea and consumed orally to support digestive health and reduce inflammation from within. However, internal use of comfrey is controversial due to its potential liver toxicity, so it's important to consult with a healthcare professional before using comfrey internally.

Coriander (Cilantro)

Origin: Coriander or cilantro belongs to the Apiaceae family. It originated in Southern Europe to Western Asia and is widely cultivated worldwide.

Application: Coriander aids digestion and supports detoxification. It can be used fresh or dried as a flavoring agent in various cuisines, including Indian, Middle Eastern, and Latin American dishes. Coriander leaves, stems, and seeds are all edible and can be added to salads, soups, stews, curries, and sauces to enhance flavor and promote digestive health. Additionally, coriander seeds can be brewed into a tea to aid digestion and promote detoxification.

Dandelion

Origin: Dandelion is a flowering plant belonging to the Asteraceae family. It has become naturalized in many parts of the world. Dandelion is widely regarded as a weed but is also valued for its culinary and medicinal properties.

Application:

Dandelion supports liver health and aids digestion. It can be consumed in various forms, including raw leaves in salads, cooked greens in soups and stir-fries, or dried roots and leaves brewed into teas or used as herbal supplements. Dandelion root tea is particularly popular for its liver-cleansing and detoxifying properties, while dandelion leaf tea can aid digestion and promote overall health.

Echinacea

Origin: Echinacea is native to North America. It commonly used as a dietary supplement for its immune-boosting properties.

Application: Echinacea boosts immune support and helps with colds. It is typically consumed in the form of teas, tinctures, capsules, or extracts made from the roots, leaves, or flowers of the echinacea plant.

Elderberry

Origin: Elderberry, derived from the Sambucus nigra plant, is a dark purple berry. Native to Europe, North Africa, and Western Asia, it is traditionally used medicine and culinary.

Application: Elderberry enhances immune support and helps with colds. It can be consumed fresh, dried, or as a syrup, tincture, or extract. Elderberry syrup is a popular remedy for colds and flu due to its high levels of antioxidants and immune-boosting properties. Elderberry supplements are also available in various forms, including capsules, gummies, and lozenges, for convenient consumption.

Elecampane

Origin: Elecampane, scientifically known as Inula helenium, is a perennial herb native to Europe and Western Asia. It has large, yellow flowers and aromatic roots that have been used in traditional medicine for centuries.

Application: Elecampane supports respiratory health and alleviates coughs. It can be consumed as a tea, tincture, or syrup made from the dried root of the elecampane plant. Elecampane tea is particularly effective for soothing coughs, clearing congestion, and promoting respiratory health. It can also be used as a natural remedy for asthma, bronchitis, and other respiratory conditions.

Evening Primrose

Origin: Evening primrose, also known as Oenothera biennis, is a biennial flowering plant native to North America. It produces bright yellow flowers that bloom in the evening, giving rise to its common name.

Application: Evening primrose is beneficial for skin health and alleviating PMS symptoms. It can be consumed in the form of oil extracted from the seeds. It can be taken orally as a dietary supplement or applied topically to the skin to moisturize, soothe inflammation, and alleviate symptoms of PMS.

Fennel

Origin: Fennel (Foeniculum vulgare), is a flowering plant belonging to the carrot family. It originated in Mediterranean region but is now cultivated worldwide for its culinary and medicinal uses.

Application: Fennel aids digestion and reduces bloating. It can be consumed in various forms, including raw or cooked bulbs, seeds, and leaves. Fennel bulbs are often sliced or chopped and used in salads, soups, stews, and stir-fries, while fennel seeds can be brewed into tea or chewed after meals to aid digestion and freshen breath. Fennel leaves can also be used as an aromatic herb in cooking or brewed into tea for digestive support.

Fenugreek

Origin: Fenugreek is an annual herb native to the Mediterranean region, Western Asia, and South Asia. It has a long history of use in culinary and medicinal applications.

Application: Fenugreek supports lactation and regulates blood sugar levels. It can be consumed in various forms, including whole seeds, ground powder, capsules, teas, and extracts. Fenugreek seeds are commonly used in cooking to add flavor and aroma to dishes, especially in Indian, Middle Eastern, and African cuisines. Fenugreek tea is often consumed by nursing mothers to stimulate milk production, while fenugreek supplements are taken to help manage blood sugar levels in individuals with diabetes or metabolic syndrome.

Garlic

Origin: Garlic, scientifically known as Allium sativum, is a bulbous plant belonging to the Alliaceae family. It is native to Central Asia and has been cultivated for thousands of years for its culinary and medicinal properties.

Application: Garlic supports heart health and boosts immune support. It can be consumed raw, cooked, or as a dietary supplement. Raw garlic cloves can be crushed or minced and added to various dishes, such as soups, sauces, stir-fries, and salads, to impart flavor and provide health benefits. Garlic supplements, including capsules, tablets, and extracts, are also available for individuals who prefer a more concentrated form of garlic for medicinal purposes.

Ginger

Origin: Ginger is a flowering plant belonging to the Zingiberaceae family. It is cultivated in tropical and subtropical regions worldwide for its culinary and medicinal uses.

Application: Ginger helps with nausea and aids digestion. It can be consumed fresh, dried, or as a supplement. Fresh ginger root can be sliced, grated, or brewed into a tea to alleviate nausea, indigestion, and motion sickness. Dried ginger powder is commonly used as a spice in cooking and baking, while ginger supplements, such as capsules, tablets, and extracts, are available for those seeking more concentrated doses of ginger for therapeutic purposes.

Ginko biloba

Origin: Ginko biloba, a unique tree is native to China. It is one of the oldest living tree species on Earth and has a long history of use in traditional Chinese medicine.

Application: Ginko biloba enhances memory and improves circulation. It is typically consumed as a dietary supplement made from ginkgo leaf extract. Ginkgo supplements are available in various forms, including capsules, tablets, and liquid extracts. They are often taken orally to support cognitive function, enhance memory, improve concentration, and boost blood circulation to the brain and extremities.

Ginseng

Origin: Ginseng refers to several species of plants belonging to the Panax genus, including Asian ginseng (Panax ginseng) and American ginseng (Panax quinquefolius). These perennial herbs are native to Eastern Asia and North America, respectively, and have been used for centuries in traditional medicine.

Application: Ginseng provides energy and boosts immune support. It is commonly consumed as a dietary supplement made from ginseng root extract. Ginseng supplements are available in various forms, including capsules, tablets, powders, and liquid extracts. They are often taken orally to enhance physical and mental energy, reduce fatigue, improve immune function, and support overall health and well-being.

Goji Berry

Origin: Goji berry, also known as wolfberry, is the fruit of the Lycium barbarum and Lycium chinense plants, which belong to the Solanaceae family. These deciduous shrubs are native to China and other parts of Asia and have been used in traditional Chinese medicine for centuries.

Application: Goji berry supports eye health and enhances immune support. It can be consumed fresh, dried, or as a juice, tea, or dietary supplement. Dried goji berries are often eaten as a snack or added to trail mixes, cereals, yogurt, and baked goods. Goji berry juice is also popular for its antioxidant properties and potential health benefits. Additionally, goji supplements, such as capsules, tablets, and extracts, are available for those seeking a more concentrated form of goji for medicinal purposes.

Goldenseal

Origin: Goldenseal, scientifically known as Hydrastis canadensis, is a perennial herb native to North America. It is commonly used in herbal supplements and natural health products.

Application: Goldenseal is effective in treating infections and boosting immune support. It is typically consumed as a dietary supplement made from goldenseal root extract. Goldenseal supplements are available in various forms, including capsules, tablets, tinctures, and teas. They are often taken orally to support immune function, treat infections, and promote overall health and well-being.

Gotu Kola

Origin: Gotu kola, scientifically known as Centella Asiatica, is native to Asia, Africa, and Oceania. It has been used for centuries in traditional medicine systems, including Ayurveda and Traditional Chinese Medicine (TCM).

Application: Gotu kola supports skin health and cognitive function. You can use it fresh, dried, or as supplements. Eat the leaves raw, cook them, or make salads, soups, and stir-fries. Dried gotu kola leaves and powder can be brewed into tea or infused into oils for topical use. Gotu kola supplements, including capsules, tablets, and extracts, are also available for those seeking a more concentrated form of gotu kola for medicinal purposes.

Hawthorn

Origin: Hawthorn is a shrub or small tree belonging to the Rosaceae family. It is native to Europe, Asia, and North America. It has several cardiovascular benefits and is used in medicine for centuries.

Application: Hawthorn supports heart health and regulates blood pressure. Hawthorn berries, leaves, and flowers are commonly used to prepare herbal remedies.. They are often taken orally to support cardiovascular health, improve circulation, lower blood pressure, and strengthen the heart muscle.

Hibiscus

Origin: Hibiscus, scientifically known as Hibiscus sabdariffa, belongs to the Malvaceae family. It grows in warm, subtropical, and tropical regions worldwide. It is cultivated for its ornamental flowers and medicinal properties.

Application: Hibiscus helps regulate blood pressure and aids digestion. It can be consumed as a tea or infusion. Hibiscus tea is enjoyed both hot and cold and is often sweetened with honey or flavored with citrus fruits. Additionally, hibiscus supplements, such as capsules, tablets, and extracts, are available for individuals seeking a more concentrated form of hibiscus for medicinal purposes.

Holy Basil (Tulsi)

Origin: Holy basil, also known as tulsi, is a sacred plant in Hinduism and is revered for its medicinal properties. It belongs to the Lamiaceae family and is native to the Indian subcontinent. Holy basil is widely used in Ayurvedic medicine and has adaptogenic, anti-inflammatory, and antioxidant properties.

Application: Holy basil reduces stress levels and supports respiratory health. It can be consumed as a tea, tincture, or powder. Holy basil leaves are commonly used to make herbal teas, often blended with other herbs for added flavor and therapeutic benefits. Holy basil supplements, including capsules, tablets, and extracts, are also available for those seeking a more convenient and concentrated form of holy basil for medicinal purposes.

Hops

Origin: Hops originated in Europe, Western Asia, and North America and is primarily cultivated for use in the brewing industry to impart bitterness, flavor, and aroma to beer.

Application: Hops aids with insomnia and anxiety. It is commonly consumed as a tea or supplement. Hops flowers, also known as hop cones, are used to prepare herbal teas and tinctures. Hops supplements, including capsules, tablets, and extracts, are available for individuals seeking the sedative and anxiolytic effects of hops for sleep support and relaxation.

Horehound

Origin: Horehound is native to Europe, North Africa, and Western Asia and has been cultivated in other parts of the world, including North America and Australia.

Application: Horehound is beneficial for coughs and respiratory health. It can be consumed as a tea, syrup, or lozenge. Horehound leaves and flowers are used to prepare herbal remedies for respiratory conditions, including coughs, bronchitis, and sore throat. Horehound supplements, such as capsules, tablets, and extracts, are also available for individuals seeking the respiratory benefits of horehound in a more convenient form.

Horsetail

Origin: Horsetail belongs to the Equisetaceae family. It is native to the Northern Hemisphere and is characterized by its jointed stems and needle-like leaves.

Application: Horsetail supports bone health and skin health. It can be consumed as a tea, tincture, or supplement. Horsetail aerial parts, including stems and leaves, are used to prepare herbal remedies for various health conditions. Horsetail tea is made by steeping dried horsetail herb in hot water, while horsetail tinctures and supplements are available in liquid extract, capsule, and tablet forms.

Jasmine

Origin: Jasmine is a fragrant flowering plant belonging to the Oleaceae family. It originated in tropical and subtropical regions of Eurasia, Oceania, and Australasia and is cultivated for its aromatic flowers, which are prized for their pleasant scent and therapeutic properties.

Application: Jasmine is known for its stress-relieving properties and its benefits for skin health. It can be used in various forms, including essential oil, tea, and topical applications. Jasmine essential oil is commonly used in aromatherapy to promote relaxation, reduce stress and anxiety, and improve mood. Jasmine tea, made from the dried flowers of the jasmine plant, is enjoyed for its soothing aroma and calming effects.

Juniper Berry

Origin: Juniper berry, scientifically known as Juniperus communis, is a small coniferous tree or shrub belonging to the Cupressaceae family. It is native to the Northern Hemisphere and is distributed throughout Europe, Asia, and North America. Juniper berries are the female seed cones of the juniper plant and are used in traditional medicine for their aromatic and medicinal properties.

Application: Juniper berry supports digestion and urinary health. It is commonly used in herbal remedies, including teas, tinctures, and extracts. Juniper berry tea is made by steeping dried juniper berries in hot water, and it is often consumed to aid digestion, relieve bloating, and promote urinary tract health. Juniper berry tinctures and extracts are also available and can be taken orally for similar therapeutic benefits.

Lavender

Origin: Lavender is a fragrant flowering plant belonging to the Lamiaceae family. It is cultivated worldwide for its aromatic flowers, which are valued for their calming and soothing properties.

Application: Lavender is known for its ability to reduce anxiety and promote relaxation, making it beneficial for managing stress and improving sleep quality. It can be used in various forms, including essential oil, herbal tea, and topical applications. Lavender tea, made from dried lavender flowers, is consumed to promote relaxation and improve sleep.

Lemon Balm

Origin: Lemon balm is native to Europe, North Africa, and West Asia and is cultivated worldwide for its aromatic leaves, which have a lemony scent and flavor.

Application: Lemon balm is known for its calming effects on the nervous system and its ability to improve digestion. Lemon balm tea is made by steeping dried lemon balm leaves in hot water, and it is consumed to promote relaxation, reduce anxiety, and aid digestion. Lemon balm tinctures and extracts are also available and can be taken orally for similar therapeutic benefits. Additionally, lemon balm essential oil can be diffused aromatically or applied topically for its calming and soothing effects.

Licorice Root

Origin: Licorice root is native to Southern Europe and parts of Asia and is cultivated for its sweet-tasting roots, which have been used in traditional medicine for thousands of years.

Application: Licorice root is known for its beneficial effects on respiratory health and digestion. It can be used in various forms, including herbal tea, decoction, and powder. Licorice root tea is made by steeping dried licorice root slices or powder in hot water, and it is consumed to soothe sore throats, relieve coughs, and support respiratory health. Licorice root decoctions, made by boiling licorice root in water, are used to treat digestive issues, including indigestion, heartburn, and ulcers. Licorice root powder can be added to herbal formulations or taken as a dietary supplement for its therapeutic effects.

Linden

Origin: Linden, also known as lime flower originated in Europe, North America, and Asia and is known for its fragrant and nectar-rich flowers.

Application: Linden has calming effects on the nervous system and its ability to provide relief from cold symptoms. Linden flower tea is made by steeping dried linden flowers in hot water, and it is consumed to promote relaxation, reduce anxiety, and alleviate cold symptoms, such as coughing and congestion. Linden tinctures and syrups are also available and can be taken orally for similar therapeutic benefits.

Marshmallow Root

Origin: Marshmallow root, scientifically known as Althaea officinalis, is a perennial herb native to Europe, Western Asia, and Northern Africa.

Application: Marshmallow root is known for its benefits for digestive and respiratory health. It can be consumed as a tea, tincture, or capsule. Marshmallow root tea is made by steeping dried marshmallow root in hot water, and it is consumed to soothe digestive issues such as indigestion, heartburn, and gastritis. It can also be used to alleviate respiratory issues like coughs, sore throats, and bronchitis. Marshmallow root tinctures and capsules are also available and can be taken orally to support digestive and respiratory health.

Milk Thistle

Origin: Milk thistle is native to the Mediterranean region and parts of Europe. It belongs to the Asteraceae family. It has liver-protective properties.

Application: It is beneficial for liver health and detoxification. It can be consumed as a tea, tincture, or capsule. Milk thistle tea is made by steeping dried milk thistle seeds or leaves in hot water, and it is consumed to support liver function and promote detoxification. Milk thistle tinctures and capsules are also available and can be taken orally to support liver health.

Moringa

Origin: Moringa is scientifically known as Moringa oleifera. It is widely cultivated for its edible parts and medicinal properties.

Application: Moringa is known for its nutrient-rich profile and anti-inflammatory properties. It can be consumed as a powder, capsule, or tea. Moringa powder is made by drying and grinding moringa leaves into a fine powder, which can be added to smoothies, soups, or beverages to boost nutrient intake and reduce inflammation. Moringa capsules and teas are also available and can be taken orally to support overall health and well-being.

Motherwort

Origin: Motherwort, scientifically known as Leonurus cardiaca, is a perennial herb native to Europe and Asia. It belongs to the Lamiaceae family and has been used for centuries in traditional medicine for its medicinal properties.

Application: Motherwort is known for its benefits for heart health and anxiety relief. It can be consumed as a tea, tincture, or capsule. Motherwort tea is made by steeping dried motherwort leaves and flowers in hot water, and it is consumed to support cardiovascular health and reduce anxiety symptoms. Motherwort tinctures and capsules are also available and can be taken orally to support heart health and promote relaxation.

Mullein

Origin: Mullein belongs to the Scrophulariaceae family and has been used for centuries in traditional medicine for its medicinal properties.

Application: Mullein is known for its benefits for respiratory health and cough relief. It can be consumed as a tea, tincture, or syrup. Mullein tinctures and syrups are also available and can be taken orally to support respiratory health and soothe cough symptoms.

Lemongrass

Origin: Lemongrass is native to tropical regions of Asia, particularly India, Sri Lanka, and Malaysia. It has been used for centuries in traditional medicine and cooking.

Lemongrass prefers warm, sunny, and humid climates, and thrives in well-draining sandy loam soil. It requires regular watering, especially during dry periods. Propagation is usually done by dividing clumps of existing plants or from seeds. It should be planted in early spring, with plants spaced about 24 inches apart.

Applications: Lemongrass is used in teas to relieve stomach discomfort and digestive problems. It contains compounds with anti-inflammatory properties and its essential oil is used in aromatherapy for its calming and relaxing effects.

Marjoram

Origin: Marjoram is native to the Mediterranean region and Western Asia. It has been used in cooking and medicine since ancient Greek and Roman times.

Marjoram prefers a warm, sunny climate and well-draining, fertile soil. It requires moderate watering, allowing the soil to dry out between watering.

Applications: Marjoram is used to relieve digestive problems such as bloating and gas. It has antibacterial and antiviral properties and is used in teas to promote relaxation and reduce stress.

Mugwort (Artemisia vulgaris)

Origin: Mugwort is native to Europe, Asia, and North Africa. It has been used in traditional medicine and rituals for centuries.

It thrives in well-draining soil and can tolerate poor soil conditions. It requires minimal watering once established. It should be planted in spring, with plants spaced about 18 inches apart.

Applications: Mugwort is used to stimulate digestion and relieve bloating. It helps regulate menstrual cycles and alleviate menstrual pain and is used in teas to promote relaxation and improve sleep quality.

Neem

Origin: Neem is native to the Indian subcontinent. It has been used in Ayurveda and traditional medicine for thousands of years.

Neem prefers hot, arid climates and well-draining, sandy soil. It requires minimal watering once established and can be grown from seeds or cuttings. It should be planted in spring or early summer, with plants spaced about 15 feet apart.

Applications: Neem is used in oils and creams to treat skin conditions like eczema and acne. Neem twigs are used as natural toothbrushes to promote oral hygiene, and its leaves and bark are used in teas to boost the immune system and fight infections.

Nettle

Origin: Nettle, scientifically known as Urtica dioica, is a perennial flowering plant native to Europe, Asia, North Africa, and North America. It belongs to the Urticaceae family and has a long history of use in traditional medicine for its medicinal properties.

Application: Nettle is known for its benefits for allergy relief and joint health. It can be consumed as a tea, tincture, or capsule. Nettle tea is made by steeping dried nettle leaves in hot water, and it is consumed to alleviate allergy symptoms such as sneezing, runny nose, and itchy eyes. Nettle tinctures and capsules are also available and can be taken orally to support joint health and reduce inflammation.

Olive Leaf

Origin: Originating from the Mediterranean region, olive leaves have been used since ancient times. Cultivation involves growing olive trees, which thrive in well-drained soil and full sun. They are primarily found in countries such as Spain, Italy, Greece, and Tunisia.

Applications: Herbal applications include use for their antioxidant, anti-inflammatory, and antimicrobial properties, often in the form of extracts or teas to support immune function and cardiovascular health.

Oregano

Origin: Oregano, scientifically known as Origanum vulgare, is a perennial herb native to the Mediterranean region. It belongs to the Lamiaceae family and has been used for centuries in traditional medicine for its medicinal properties.

Application: Oregano is known for its benefits for immune support and respiratory health. It can be consumed as a dried herb, essential oil, or capsule. Oregano essential oil can be diffused in the air or diluted and applied topically to support respiratory health and boost immune function. Oregano capsules are also available and can be taken orally to support overall health and well-being.

Parsley

Origin: Parsley, scientifically known as Petroselinum crispum, is a biennial herb native to the Mediterranean region. It belongs to the Apiaceae family and has been used for centuries in traditional medicine for its medicinal properties.

Application: Parsley is known for its benefits for digestion and detoxification. It can be consumed as a fresh herb, dried herb, or tea. Parsley tea is made by steeping fresh or dried parsley leaves in hot water, and it is consumed to aid digestion and support detoxification processes. Fresh parsley can also be added to salads, soups, and other dishes to enhance flavor and promote digestive health.

Passionflower

Origin: Passionflower, scientifically known as Passiflora incarnata, is a climbing vine native to the southeastern United States. It belongs to the Passifloraceae family and has been used for centuries in traditional medicine for its calming and sedative properties.

Application: Passionflower is known for its benefits for insomnia and anxiety relief. It can be consumed as a tea, tincture, or capsule. Passionflower tea is made by steeping dried passionflower leaves and flowers in hot water, and it is consumed to promote relaxation and improve sleep quality. Passionflower tinctures and capsules are also available and can be taken orally to reduce anxiety symptoms and promote overall well-being.

Peppermint

Origin: Peppermint, scientifically known as Mentha piperita, is a hybrid mint plant native to Europe and the Middle East.

Application: Peppermint is known for its benefits for digestion and headache relief. It can be consumed as a fresh herb, dried herb, tea, or essential oil. It is consumed to reduce digestive issues such as bloating, gas, and indigestion. Peppermint essential oil can be diffused in the air or diluted and applied topically to the temples to relieve headaches and promote relaxation.

Plantain

Origin: Plantain, scientifically known as Plantago major, is a perennial herb native to Europe and parts of Asia, but it is now found worldwide. It belongs to the Plantaginaceae family and has a long history of use in traditional medicine for its various health benefits.

Application: Plantain is known for its benefits for skin health and inflammation. It can be used topically as a poultice or salve to soothe minor skin irritations, such as insect bites, rashes, and minor wounds. To make a plantain poultice, fresh plantain leaves are crushed or chewed to release their juices and then applied directly to the affected area. Plantain can also be infused with oil and used to make a healing salve. Additionally, plantain leaves can be brewed into tea and consumed to reduce inflammation and promote overall skin health.

Psyllium

Origin: Psyllium, also known as Plantago psyllium or Plantago ovata, is a plant native to Iran and India. It belongs to the Plantaginaceae family and has been used for centuries in traditional medicine for its medicinal properties.

Application: Psyllium is known for its benefits for digestive health and constipation relief. It is commonly consumed as a dietary supplement in the form of psyllium husk or psyllium powder. Psyllium husk is a soluble fiber derived from the seeds of the Plantago plant, and it is often mixed with water or juice and consumed as a laxative to relieve constipation and promote regular bowel movements. Psyllium powder can also be added to smoothies, yogurt, or baked goods to increase fiber intake and support digestive health.Pau d'Arco

Origin: It is found in the Amazon rainforest and other tropical regions of South and Central America. Cultivation requires a warm, humid climate and well-drained soil. It is predominantly found in Brazil, Argentina, and other parts of South America.

Applications: It is used as an antifungal, antibacterial, and antiviral agent. Its most common use is boosting immunity and treating infections.

Pennyroyal

Origin: Originally from Europe, North Africa, and parts of Asia, pennyroyal is a member of the mint family. It is cultivated in well-drained soil with full to partial sunlight. Locations where it is commonly found include the United States, particularly in the eastern regions, and across Europe.

Applications: It is used as a digestive aid, to relieve colds, and as a natural insect repellent. Caution is advised due to its potential toxicity.

Pine Bark

Origin: Sourced from the bark of certain species of pine trees, notably the maritime pine (Pinus pinaster), it has a historical origin in the Mediterranean region. Cultivation involves managing pine forests, often in coastal areas with sandy soil. Pine bark is found in places like France, Spain, and North America.

Applications: Herbal applications include its use for its antioxidant properties, to support cardiovascular health, improve circulation, and reduce inflammation.

Red Clover

Origin: Red clover, scientifically known as Trifolium pratense, is a perennial flowering plant native to Europe, Western Asia, and Northwest Africa. It belongs to the Fabaceae family and has a long history of use in traditional medicine for its various health benefits.

Application: Red clover is known for its benefits for menopause and skin health. It can be consumed as a tea, tincture, or capsule. Red clover tea is made by steeping dried red clover flowers in hot water, and it is consumed to alleviate menopausal symptoms such as hot flashes, night sweats, and mood swings. Red clover tinctures and capsules are also available and can be taken orally to support overall health and well-being. Additionally, red clover can be applied topically as a cream or ointment to soothe skin conditions such as eczema, psoriasis, and acne.

Reishi Mushroom

Origin: It is a fungus that grows on various types of trees. It belongs to the Ganodermataceae family and has several uses in traditional medicine for centuries.

Application: Reishi mushroom is known for its benefits for immune support and stress relief. It can be consumed as a tea, tincture, or capsule. Reishi mushroom tea is made by boiling dried reishi mushroom slices in water, and it is consumed to boost immune function and reduce stress levels. Reishi mushroom tinctures and capsules are also available and can be taken orally to support overall health and well-being. Additionally, reishi mushroom extracts can be added to soups, smoothies, or other recipes to enhance flavor and provide health benefits.

Rosemary

Origin: Rosemary, scientifically known as Rosmarinus officinalis, is an evergreen shrub native to the Mediterranean region. It belongs to the Lamiaceae family and has been used for centuries in traditional medicine for its medicinal properties.

Application: Rosemary is known for its benefits for memory and digestion. It can be consumed as tea, used as a culinary herb in cooking, or applied topically as an essential oil. Rosemary tea is made by steeping dried rosemary leaves in hot water, and it is consumed to improve memory and cognitive function. Rosemary essential oil can be diffused in the air or diluted with carrier oil and applied to the skin to promote digestion and alleviate digestive discomfort. Additionally, fresh or dried rosemary leaves can be used to flavor various dishes, such as roasted vegetables, meats, and soups, to aid digestion and enhance flavor.

Red Raspberry Leaf

Origin: Originating from Europe and parts of Asia, red raspberry leaves come from the raspberry plant. Cultivation involves growing raspberry bushes, which prefer well-drained soil and full sun. They are commonly found in temperate regions, including North America, Europe, and Asia.

Applications: It is used as a uterine tonic, to ease menstrual discomfort, support pregnancy, and improve overall reproductive health.

Rhodiola

Origin: Native to the cold regions of Europe and Asia, particularly in mountainous areas, Rhodiola grows wild in high-altitude locations. Cultivation requires well-drained soil and a cold climate, often in rocky terrain. It is found in countries like Russia, China, and Mongolia.

Applications: It is used as an adaptogen to reduce stress, enhance mental performance, and combat fatigue.

Shepherd's Purse

Origin: Originating from Europe, the shepherd's purse is now found worldwide. It grows in various soils and conditions, often in disturbed grounds like roadsides and fields. Locations include North America, Europe, and Asia.

Applications: It is used to stop bleeding, treat wounds, and alleviate heavy menstrual bleeding due to its astringent and styptic properties.

Spirulina

Origin: This blue-green algae originates from alkaline lakes in Africa and Central and South America. Cultivation involves growing in controlled environments, such as open ponds or closed-loop systems, with warm temperatures and plenty of sunlight. It is found in regions with suitable growing conditions, such as parts of Africa, Asia, and the Americas.

Applications: It is used as a nutrient-dense supplement rich in protein, vitamins, minerals, and antioxidants, often used to boost energy, improve immune function, and support overall health.

Saffron

Origin: Saffron is believed to have originated in the region of Greece, specifically on the island of Crete. It has been cultivated for over 3,000 years and was first domesticated in or near Greece.

Saffron thrives in Mediterranean climates with hot and dry summers and cold winters. Saffron is primarily cultivated in regions with a suitable climate, including Iran, India, Spain, Greece, and Italy.

Applications: Saffron is highly prized as a spice, adding a unique flavor, aroma, and vibrant yellow color to dishes such as paella, risotto, and bouillabaisse. Saffron has been used in various cultures for its medicinal properties. Saffron is sometimes used in aromatherapy for its calming and mood-enhancing properties. Due to its antioxidant properties, saffron is used in skincare products for its potential benefits in promoting healthy and glowing skin. Modern research suggests that saffron may help improve mood, reduce symptoms of PMS, aid in weight loss, enhance memory, and support eye health.

Sage

Origin: Sage, scientifically known as Salvia officinalis, is a perennial herb native to the Mediterranean region. It belongs to the Lamiaceae family and has a long history of use in traditional medicine for its various health benefits.

Application: Sage is known for its benefits for memory and throat health. It can be consumed as tea, used as a culinary herb in cooking, or applied topically as an essential oil. Sage tea is made by steeping dried sage leaves in hot water, and it is consumed to improve memory and cognitive function. Sage essential oil can be diffused in the air or diluted with a carrier oil and applied to the skin to promote throat health and alleviate sore throat symptoms. Additionally, fresh or dried sage leaves can be used to flavor various dishes, such as sauces, stuffings, and marinades, to aid digestion and enhance flavor.

Saw Palmetto

Origin: Saw palmetto, scientifically known as Serenoa repens, is a small palm native to the southeastern United States. It belongs to the Arecaceae family and has been used for centuries in traditional medicine for its medicinal properties.

Application: Saw palmetto is known for its benefits for prostate health and urinary health. It is commonly consumed as a dietary supplement. Saw palmetto supplements are made from the berries of the saw palmetto plant, and they are taken orally to support prostate health and alleviate symptoms of benign prostatic hyperplasia (BPH), such as urinary frequency, urgency, and nocturia. Additionally, saw palmetto extracts can be added to prostate health formulas or combined with other herbs to enhance their effectiveness.

Schisandra

Origin: Schisandra, scientifically known as Schisandra chinensis, is a woody vine native to East Asia.

Application: Schisandra is known for its benefits for liver health and stress relief. It is commonly consumed as a dietary supplement in the form of capsules, tablets, or extracts. Schisandra supplements are made from the dried berries of the Schisandra plant, and they are taken orally to support liver function and promote overall health and well-being. Schisandra extracts can also be added to teas, tinctures, or other herbal formulations to enhance their liver-protective and adaptogenic properties. Additionally, fresh or dried Schisandra berries can be brewed into tea and consumed to reduce stress levels and promote relaxation.

Slippery Elm

Origin: Slippery elm is native to North America.

Application: Slippery elm is known for its benefits for digestive health and throat health. It is commonly consumed as a tea, powder, or lozenge. Slippery elm tea is made by steeping dried slippery elm bark in hot water, and it is consumed to soothe digestive discomforts, such as heartburn, indigestion, and diarrhea. Slippery elm powder can be mixed with water or juice and consumed as a thick paste to coat the throat and alleviate sore throat symptoms. Slippery elm lozenges are also available and can be sucked on to relieve coughs and throat irritation. Additionally, slippery elm supplements are available in capsule or tablet form and can be taken orally to support digestive health and promote overall well-being.

Spearmint

Origin: Spearmint is scientifically known as Mentha spicata. It is native to Europe and Asia. It is widely cultivated for its culinary and medicinal uses.

Application: Spearmint is known for its benefits for digestion and respiratory health. It can be consumed as tea, used as a culinary herb in cooking, or applied topically as an essential oil. Spearmint tea is made by steeping fresh or dried spearmint leaves in hot water, and it is consumed to promote digestion, alleviate indigestion, and soothe stomach discomfort. Spearmint essential oil can be diffused in the air or diluted with carrier oil and applied to the skin to relieve respiratory congestion and promote clear breathing. Additionally, fresh spearmint leaves can be used to flavor various dishes, such as salads, beverages, and desserts, to aid digestion and enhance flavor.

St. John's Wort

Origin: St. John's Wort, scientifically known as Hypericum perforatum, is a perennial herb native to Europe and Asia. It belongs to the Hypericaceae family and has been used for centuries in traditional medicine for its medicinal properties.

Application: St. John's Wort is known for its benefits for depression and nerve pain. It is commonly consumed as a tea, taken in capsule or tablet form, or applied topically as an oil or cream.. St. John's Wort supplements are available over-the-counter and can be taken orally to support mental health and well-being. St. John's Wort oil or cream can be applied topically to the skin to relieve nerve pain, such as sciatica, neuralgia, and muscle aches. However, it is essential to consult with a healthcare professional before using St. John's Wort, especially if you are taking other medications, as it may interact with certain drugs.

Thyme

Origin: Thyme, scientifically known as Thymus vulgaris, is a perennial herb native to the Mediterranean region. It belongs to the Lamiaceae family and has been used for centuries in traditional medicine for its medicinal properties.

Application: Thyme is known for its benefits for respiratory health and digestion. It can be consumed as tea, used as a culinary herb in cooking, or applied topically as an essential oil. Thyme tea is made by steeping fresh or dried thyme leaves in hot water, and it is consumed to relieve coughs, sore throats, and respiratory congestion. Thyme essential oil can be diffused in the air or diluted with a carrier oil and applied to the skin to promote respiratory health and alleviate respiratory symptoms. Additionally, fresh thyme leaves can be used to flavor various dishes, such as soups, stews, sauces, and marinades, to aid digestion and enhance flavor.

Turmeric

Origin: Turmeric, scientifically known as Curcuma longa, is a perennial herbaceous plant native to South Asia. It belongs to the Zingiberaceae family and has been used for centuries in traditional medicine for its medicinal properties.

Application: Turmeric is known for its benefits for inflammation and joint health. It can be consumed as a spice, used in cooking, or taken as a dietary supplement. Turmeric powder is derived from the dried rhizomes of the turmeric plant and is commonly used as a spice in various cuisines, such as Indian, Thai, and Middle Eastern cuisine. It can be added to curries, soups, stews, rice dishes, and beverages to impart a vibrant color and earthy flavor. Turmeric supplements are available in capsule or tablet form and can be taken orally to reduce inflammation, alleviate joint pain, and support overall health and well-being. Additionally, turmeric can be mixed with other ingredients, such as black pepper and ginger, to enhance its absorption and effectiveness.

Uva Ursi

Origin: Uva Ursi, also known as bearberry, is a perennial shrub native to North America, Europe, and Asia. It belongs to the Ericaceae family and has been used for centuries in traditional medicine for its medicinal properties.

Application: Uva Ursi is known for its benefits for urinary health and bladder infections. Uva Ursi supplements are available over-the-counter and can be taken orally to support urinary health, prevent recurrent bladder infections, and promote overall well-being. However, it is essential to consult with a healthcare professional before using Uva Ursi, especially if you are pregnant, breastfeeding, or taking other medications, as it may interact with certain drugs and have potential side effects.

Valerian

Origin: Valerian, scientifically known as Valeriana officinalis, is a perennial flowering plant native to Europe and Asia. It belongs to the Valerianaceae family and has been used for centuries in traditional medicine for its sedative and anxiolytic properties.

Application: Valerian is known for its benefits for insomnia and anxiety. It is commonly consumed as a tea, taken in capsule or tablet form, or applied topically as an essential oil. Valerian tea is made by steeping dried Valerian root in hot water, and it is consumed to promote relaxation, improve sleep quality, and alleviate symptoms of anxiety and stress. Valerian supplements are available over-the-counter and can be taken orally to support mental health and well-being. Valerian essential oil can be diffused in the air or diluted with carrier oil and applied to the skin to promote relaxation and induce restful sleep.

Vervain

Origin: Vervain, scientifically known as Verbena officinalis, is a perennial herbaceous plant native to Europe and Asia. It belongs to the Verbenaceae family and has been used for centuries in traditional medicine for its medicinal properties.

Application: Vervain is known for its benefits for nervous system support and stress relief. It can be consumed as a tea, taken in tincture or capsule form, or applied topically as a cream or ointment. Vervain tea is made by steeping dried Vervain leaves and flowers in hot water, and it is consumed to promote relaxation, reduce anxiety, and alleviate symptoms of stress and tension. Vervain tincture or capsules can be taken orally to support mental health and well-being. Additionally, Vervain cream or ointment can be applied topically to the skin to relieve muscle tension, headaches, and nervousness.

Vetiver

Origin: Vetiver also known as khus, is a perennial grass native to India. Its name "vetiver" is derived from the Tamil word "vetiver," meaning "root that is dug up." Over time, vetiver has spread to other tropical regions, including Southeast Asia, the Caribbean, West Africa, and South America.

Vetiver is a hardy plant that thrives in a wide range of soil types, from sandy to clayey, and can tolerate drought. It is typically grown in tropical and subtropical climates.

Applications: Vetiver has a variety of uses, particularly in traditional medicine and aromatherapy. Vetiver essential oil is highly valued for its calming and grounding properties. It is often used in aromatherapy to reduce stress, anxiety, and insomnia. The oil has a rich, earthy aroma that is said to promote emotional balance and relaxation. Vetiver oil has antiseptic and anti-inflammatory properties, making it beneficial for skin care. It is used to treat acne, wounds, and scars, and is known for its ability to rejuvenate aging skin. Vetiver oil is used in hair care products for its ability to strengthen hair and promote healthy growth. It is also effective in treating dandruff and dry scalp. In medicine, vetiver root infusions are used to treat digestive issues such as indigestion and stomach cramps. The cooling properties of vetiver also make it useful for managing heat-related ailments. Vetiver is used to alleviate respiratory conditions like coughs and bronchitis. Vetiver root extracts are used to reduce inflammation and relieve pain, making it beneficial for conditions like arthritis and muscle aches.

Watercress

Origin: Watercress, scientifically known as Nasturtium officinale, is a perennial aquatic plant native to Europe and Asia. It belongs to the Brassicaceae family and has been used for centuries in traditional medicine for its medicinal properties.

Application: Watercress is known for its benefits for respiratory health and nutrient support. It can be consumed raw in salads, sandwiches, and smoothies or cooked in soups, stews, and stir-fries. Watercress is rich in vitamins, minerals, antioxidants, and phytonutrients, such as vitamin C, vitamin K, vitamin A, calcium, iron, and iodine, which support immune function, promote respiratory health, and protect against oxidative stress and inflammation. Additionally, watercress can be juiced or blended into green drinks and consumed as a nutrient-dense beverage to enhance overall health and well-being.

White Willow Bark

Origin: White Willow Bark, scientifically known as Salix alba, is the bark of the white willow tree native to Europe, Asia, and North Africa. It has been used for centuries in traditional medicine for its analgesic and anti-inflammatory properties.

Application: White Willow Bark is known for its benefits for pain relief and inflammation. It can be consumed as a tea, taken in tincture or capsule form, or applied topically as a poultice or compress. White Willow Bark tea is made by steeping dried White Willow Bark in hot water, and it is consumed to alleviate symptoms of pain, such as headaches, muscle aches, and menstrual cramps, and reduce inflammation associated with arthritis, gout, and other inflammatory conditions. White Willow Bark tincture or capsules can be taken orally to relieve pain and inflammation and promote overall well-being. Additionally, White Willow Bark poultice or compress can be applied topically to the affected area to reduce swelling, soothe sore muscles, and promote healing.

Witch Hazel

Origin: Witch Hazel, scientifically known as Hamamelis virginiana, is a shrub native to North America and parts of Asia. It belongs to the Hamamelidaceae family and has been used for centuries in traditional medicine for its medicinal properties.

Application: Witch Hazel is known for its benefits for skin health and inflammation. It is commonly used as a topical treatment in the form of a liquid extract, lotion, or cream. Witch Hazel extract can be applied directly to the skin to soothe irritation, reduce redness, and alleviate symptoms of inflammation, such as itching, swelling, and discomfort. It is often used to treat minor skin conditions, including acne, eczema, psoriasis, sunburn, insect bites, and rashes.

Yarrow

Origin: Yarrow, scientifically known as Achillea millefolium, is a perennial herb native to Europe, Asia, and North America. It belongs to the Asteraceae family and has been used for centuries in traditional medicine for its medicinal properties.

Application: Yarrow is known for its benefits for wound healing and digestion. It can be consumed as a tea, taken in tincture or capsule form, or applied topically as a poultice or ointment. Yarrow tea is made by steeping dried Yarrow flowers and leaves in hot water, and it is consumed to promote digestion, relieve gastrointestinal discomfort, and alleviate symptoms of indigestion, bloating, and gas. Yarrow tincture or capsules can be taken orally to support digestive health and well-being. Additionally, Yarrow poultice or ointment can be applied topically to wounds, cuts, and bruises to promote healing, reduce inflammation, and prevent infection.

Yellow Dock

Origin: Yellow Dock, scientifically known as Rumex crispus, is a perennial herb native to Europe, Asia, and North America. It belongs to the Polygonaceae family and has been used for centuries in traditional medicine for its medicinal properties.

Application: Yellow Dock is known for its benefits for liver health and skin issues. It can be consumed as a tea, taken in tincture or capsule form, or applied topically as a poultice or salve. Yellow Dock tea is made by steeping dried Yellow Dock roots in hot water, and it is consumed to support liver function, promote detoxification, and alleviate symptoms of liver congestion, such as fatigue, bloating, and skin problems. Yellow Dock tincture or capsules can be taken orally to support liver health, improve digestion, and purify the blood.

Yellow Gentian

Origin: Yellow Gentian, also known as Gentiana lutea, is native to the mountainous regions of central and southern Europe. It is commonly found in the Alps, the Pyrenees, and the Balkan mountains.

Yellow Gentian prefer a cool, mountainous climate. It thrives in areas with full sun to partial shade and requires a cold period to germinate. The plant grows best in well-drained, slightly acidic to neutral soils. It is often found in alpine meadows and rocky soils. Propagation is typically done through seeds, which should be sown in the fall or spring.

Application: The bitter compounds in Yellow Gentian, such as gentiopicrin and amelogenin, stimulate the production of digestive enzymes and bile, aiding digestion and appetite stimulation. It is traditionally used as a general tonic to improve overall vitality and health. Historically it was used to reduce fevers and treat infections. It contains anti-inflammatory properties that can help alleviate conditions like arthritis and gout. It is often used in herbal medicine to support liver function and detoxification. The roots of Yellow Gentian have been used externally to promote wound healing and treat skin infections.

Yerba Mate

Origin: Yerba Mate, scientifically known as Ilex paraguariensis, is a species of holly native to South America, particularly Argentina, Brazil, Paraguay, and Uruguay. It belongs to the Aquifoliaceae family and has been used for centuries by indigenous tribes in South America for its stimulating and medicinal properties.

Application: Yerba Mate is known for its benefits for energy and mental focus. It is commonly consumed as a brewed beverage, known as mate or chimarrão, and enjoyed for its invigorating effects and rich flavor. Yerba Mate leaves are dried, ground into a fine powder, and steeped in hot water to make a stimulating herbal tea. It contains caffeine and other bioactive compounds, such as theobromine and polyphenols, which provide a natural energy boost, enhance mental alertness, and improve cognitive function. Yerba Mate can be enjoyed hot or cold and is often consumed socially in South American countries as a traditional beverage to promote vitality, mental clarity, and social bonding.

Yohimbe

Origin: Yohimbe is native to Central and West Africa, particularly Nigeria, Cameroon, Gabon, and Congo. It belongs to the Rubiaceae family and has been used for centuries in traditional African medicine for its medicinal properties.

Application: Yohimbe is known for its benefits for sexual health and energy. It is commonly consumed as a dietary supplement in the form of capsules, tablets, or liquid extracts. Yohimbe supplements contain the active compound yohimbine, which is derived from the bark of the Yohimbe tree and has been studied for its aphrodisiac effects and potential to improve erectile function and sexual performance in men. Yohimbe supplements are often used to treat erectile dysfunction, enhance libido, and increase sexual stamina and arousal. However, it is important to use Yohimbe supplements cautiously and under the guidance of a healthcare professional, as they may cause side effects and interact with certain medications.

Yucca

Origin: Yucca, scientifically known as Yucca schidigera, is a perennial plant native to the deserts of the southwestern United States and Mexico. It belongs to the Asparagaceae family and has been utilized for centuries by Native American tribes for its various medicinal properties.

Application: Yucca is esteemed for its benefits in promoting joint health and reducing inflammation. It is often consumed orally as a dietary supplement, typically available in capsule or tablet form. Yucca supplements are believed to help alleviate symptoms associated with arthritis, such as joint pain, stiffness, and swelling, due to its natural anti-inflammatory properties. Additionally, some individuals incorporate Yucca extract into their diet by adding it to smoothies or consuming it in powdered form. While research on the effectiveness of Yucca for joint health is ongoing, many people find relief from incorporating it into their wellness regimen.

Zedoary

Origin: Zedoary, scientifically known as Curcuma zedoaria, is a perennial herbaceous plant native to Southeast Asia and the Indian subcontinent. It belongs to the Zingiberaceae family and has been utilized for centuries in traditional Ayurvedic and Chinese medicine for its therapeutic properties.

Application: Zedoary is renowned for its benefits in promoting digestive health and reducing inflammation. It can be consumed in various forms, including fresh, dried, powdered, or as an extract. Zedoary is often used as a culinary spice in Asian cuisine, adding flavor and aroma to dishes while also offering potential health benefits. Additionally, Zedoary powder can be incorporated into herbal remedies, teas, or tinctures to support gastrointestinal function and soothe digestive discomfort. Its anti-inflammatory properties make it a valuable ingredient in natural remedies for conditions such as indigestion, bloating, and abdominal pain.

Ziziphus

Origin: Ziziphus, also known as jujube or Chinese date, encompasses several species of deciduous shrubs and small trees within the Ziziphus genus. Native to regions of Asia, Europe, and Africa, these plants belong to the Rhamnaceae family and have a long history of use in traditional medicine systems.

Application: Ziziphus is esteemed for its potential as a sleep aid and anxiety reliever. The fruit of the Ziziphus plant is often consumed raw, dried, or in the form of tea. Rich in compounds like flavonoids and saponins, Ziziphus possesses mild sedative properties that may help alleviate symptoms of anxiety and stress, promoting a sense of calmness and tranquility. Ziziphus tea is prepared by steeping dried Ziziphus fruit or leaves in hot water, creating a soothing herbal infusion that can be enjoyed before bedtime to support restful sleep and relaxation.

Chapter 5
Herbal Remedies for Common Ailments

In this chapter, you will learn about herbal remedies for addressing common health issues. From digestive issues to skin conditions, stress, and beyond, numerous herbs can provide relief and support for everyday health concerns. Below, we explore some of the most prevalent health issues and the corresponding herbal remedies that may offer relief.

Digestive Issues

Peppermint: Known for its soothing properties, peppermint can help alleviate symptoms of indigestion, bloating, and gas (Collins, 2014).

Ginger: With its anti-nausea and digestive stimulant properties, ginger is often used to ease stomach discomfort and promote healthy digestion (Collins, 2014).

Fennel: Fennel seeds contain compounds that can aid digestion, reduce bloating, and relieve gas (Collins, 2014).

Respiratory Problems

Eucalyptus: Eucalyptus leaves contain cineole, a compound known for its decongestant and expectorant properties, making it effective in easing respiratory congestion. (Groves, n.d.)

Thyme: Thyme is rich in volatile oils with antimicrobial properties, making it beneficial for treating respiratory infections and soothing coughs (Groves, n.d.).

Mullein: Mullein leaves have mucilage content that helps soothe irritation in the respiratory tract, making it useful for addressing coughs and bronchitis. (Groves, n.d.)

Skin Conditions

Calendula: Calendula flowers have anti-inflammatory and antimicrobial properties, making them effective in treating various skin conditions. It can treat cuts, burns, and rashes. (Chilukoti, 2015).

Chamomile: Chamomile possesses soothing and anti-inflammatory properties that can help alleviate skin irritation, eczema, and dermatitis.

Aloe Vera: Aloe vera gel contains compounds that promote skin healing and hydration, making it beneficial for soothing sunburns, minor cuts, and wounds.

Stress and Anxiety

Lavender: Lavender has calming properties that can help reduce stress, anxiety, and promote relaxation. (Richards, 2023)

Lemon Balm: Lemon balm contains compounds that calms the nerves, reduces anxiety, and helps in insomnia (Kelsey Kunik, 2022).

Passionflower: Passionflower is known for its sedative properties, making it effective in reducing anxiety, nervousness, and promoting relaxation. (Kelsey Kunik, 2022).

Sleep Troubles

Valerian: Valerian root has sedative properties that can help improve sleep quality and alleviate insomnia.

Chamomile: Chamomile tea promotes relaxation and improving sleep quality.

Hops: Hops contain compounds that have mild sedative effects, making them beneficial for promoting restful sleep.

Cardiovascular Health

Hawthorn: Hawthorn can help support heart health by improving circulation and lowering blood pressure.

Garlic: Garlic has cardiovascular benefits, including lowering cholesterol and blood pressure levels.

Ginger: Ginger can help improve circulation and reduce inflammation, benefiting cardiovascular health.

Women's Health

Red Raspberry Leaf: Red raspberry leaf can help support women's reproductive health and ease menstrual cramps.

Black Cohosh: Black cohosh can help alleviate symptoms of menopause, such as hot flashes and mood swings.

Chasteberry: Chasteberry can help balance hormones and alleviate symptoms of PMS and menstrual irregularities.

Men's Health

Saw Palmetto: Saw palmetto supports prostate health. It helps in reducing the symptoms of benign prostatic hyperplasia (BPH).

Ginseng: Ginseng can help improve energy levels, libido, and overall vitality in men.

Nettle: Nettle can help support prostate health and improve urinary symptoms associated with BPH.

Children's Health

Fennel: Fennel can help relieve digestive issues like colic, gas, and bloating in infants and children.

Catnip: Catnip has calming properties and can help soothe fussy babies and alleviate digestive discomfort.

Chamomile: Chamomile can help calm children and promote better sleep, as well as alleviate digestive issues.

Chapter 6
Herbs for Various Medical Conditions

As discussed in previous sections, herbs are beneficial for various medical conditions. This chapter is all about exploring those benefits along with the usage guidelines for each herb for better results.

1. Cardiovascular Diseases

Cardiovascular diseases (CVDs) include a range of conditions affecting the heart and blood vessels, such as coronary artery disease, heart failure, high blood pressure, and stroke. These ailments can stem from various factors like elevated cholesterol, hypertension, diabetes, obesity, smoking, and sedentary lifestyles. Prioritizing cardiovascular health is essential for averting complications and enhancing overall well-being. Notable herbs known for their cardiovascular support include hawthorn, garlic, and ginko biloba.

Hawthorn

Hawthorn, a botanical remedy cherished for centuries, is renowned for fortifying heart health and addressing cardiovascular concerns. Packed with antioxidants, flavonoids, and other bioactive compounds, hawthorn increases vasodilation, bolsters blood flow, and fortifies cardiac muscle. Its anti-inflammatory attributes mitigate vessel inflammation and regulate blood pressure. (Nick H. Mashour, 1998). Moreover, hawthorn's cholesterol-regulating properties deter arterial plaque accumulation.

Usage Guidelines for Hawthorn

Preparation: Prepare hawthorn tea by steeping 1 to 2 teaspoons of dried hawthorn berries or leaves in hot water for 10 to 15 minutes. Alternatively, take hawthorn supplements as directed by the manufacturer.

Dosage: Consume hawthorn tea or supplements twice daily for optimal cardiovascular support.

Application: Drink hawthorn tea between meals or as part of your daily routine. If using supplements, take them with water after meals.

Duration: Consistently use hawthorn for several weeks to experience its full benefits for heart health.

Garlic

Garlic, extensively researched for its multifaceted benefits, extends significant support to cardiovascular health. Laced with sulfur compounds like allicin, it wields antioxidant and anti-inflammatory prowess, curtailing blood pressure, diminishing cholesterol, and thwarting clot formation. It promotes circulation and stops atherosclerosis progression. Regular garlic consumption can mitigate heart disease and stroke risks (Suman Ray, 2021).

Usage Guidelines for Garlic:

Preparation: Incorporate fresh garlic into your daily meals by crushing or chopping it and adding it to salads, soups, or cooked dishes. Alternatively, take Garlic supplements as directed by the manufacturer.

Dosage: Consume 1 to 2 cloves of fresh garlic per day or follow the recommended dosage of Garlic supplements for cardiovascular support.

Application: Use fresh garlic in cooking or swallow garlic supplements with water after meals.

Duration: Incorporate garlic into your daily routine for long-term cardiovascular health benefits.

Ginko Biloba

Ginko biloba, steeped in historical significance for cognitive enhancement, also merits recognition for cardiovascular well-being. Flowing with flavonoids and terpenoids, it boosts blood circulation, increases vasodilation, and stops inflammation. The herb's antiplatelet properties discourage clot formation, mitigating heart attack and stroke risks, while its antioxidants shield vessels from free radical harm (Suman Ray, 2021).

Usage Guidelines for Ginko biloba:

Preparation: Take ginko biloba supplements as directed by the manufacturer, usually with water after meals.

Dosage: Follow the recommended dosage of Ginko biloba supplements for cardiovascular support.

Application: Swallow ginko biloba supplements whole with water, preferably after meals.

Duration: Consistently use ginko biloba supplements according to the recommended dosage for sustained cardiovascular benefits.

2. Neurological Disorders

Neurological disorders include a broad spectrum of conditions affecting the nervous system, including the brain, spinal cord, and peripheral nerves. These disorders can affect in various ways, such as cognitive impairment, mood disturbances, movement disorders, and sensory deficits. Herbs like ginko biloba, St. John's wort, and bacopa have garnered attention for their potential to support neurological health and alleviate symptoms associated with neurological conditions.

Ginko biloba

Ginko biloba, derived from the leaves of the ginkgo tree, is esteemed for its neuroprotective properties and cognitive-enhancing effects. Rich in flavonoids and terpenoids, ginko biloba promotes cerebral circulation, augments oxygen and nutrient delivery to brain cells, and mitigates oxidative stress. These mechanisms contribute to improved cognitive function, memory retention, and mental clarity. Additionally, Ginko biloba's anti-inflammatory properties may aid in the management of neurodegenerative disorders (R.V.Anand, 2023).

Usage Guidelines for Ginko biloba:

Preparation: Take Ginko biloba supplements in the form of capsules or tablets.

Dosage: For effective end efficient results follow the recommended dosage on packaging..

Application: Swallow Ginko biloba supplements with water, preferably after meals to enhance absorption.

Duration: Consistently use Ginko biloba supplements according to the recommended dosage for optimal neurological benefits over time.

St. John's Wort

St. John's Wort, a flowering plant native to Europe, has gained recognition for its antidepressant properties and mood-stabilizing effects. Its active constituents, including hypericin and hyperforin, modulate neurotransmitter levels in the brain, particularly serotonin, dopamine, and norepinephrine, thereby alleviating symptoms of depression, anxiety, and mood disorders. St. John's Wort also exhibits anti-inflammatory and neuroprotective actions, which may contribute to its therapeutic efficacy in neurological conditions.

Usage Guidelines for St. John's Wort:

Preparation: Take St. John's Wort supplements in the form of standardized extracts, capsules, or tinctures.

Dosage: Contact health care professionals dealing with herbal medicines to find out exactly how much dosage is required for you depending on age and other conditions.

Application: Ingest St. John's Wort supplements with water, ideally after meals to facilitate absorption and minimize gastrointestinal discomfort.

Duration: Use St. John's Wort supplements consistently according to the recommended dosage for sustained neurological benefits.

Bacopa

Bacopa monnieri, an adaptogenic herb native to India, is esteemed for its cognitive-enhancing and neuroprotective properties. Its bioactive constituents, known as bacosides, bolster synaptic communication, enhance neurotransmitter function, and stimulate neuronal regeneration, thereby enhancing cognitive function, memory retention, and learning capacity. Bacopa also exerts antioxidant and anti-inflammatory effects, which may counteract neuronal damage and mitigate neurodegenerative processes.

Usage Guidelines for Bacopa:

Preparation: Take the prepared supplements of bacopa and consume them according to the mentioned dosage.

Dosage:

For Children (6-12 years) use100-200 mg per day of a standardized bacopa extract. For age 13-18 years use 200-300 mg per day.

For Adults (19-64 years) you can use 300-450 mg per day.

Seniors with age 65+ years can use 300 mg per day of a standardized Bacopa extract.

Application: Ingest Bacopa supplements with water, preferably after meals for optimal absorption and tolerance.

Duration: Incorporate Bacopa supplements into your daily regimen and adhere to the recommended dosage for sustained neurological benefits over time.

3. Gastrointestinal and Digestive Disorders

Gastrointestinal (GI) and digestive disorders include a range of conditions affecting the digestive tract, including the stomach, intestines, liver, and pancreas. These disorders can cause symptoms such as abdominal pain, bloating, gas, diarrhea, constipation, and indigestion. Herbs like Peppermint, Fennel, and Ginger have been traditionally used to alleviate symptoms associated with GI and digestive disorders and promote overall digestive health

Peppermint

Peppermint, derived from the Mentha piperita plant, is prized for its soothing properties and ability to relieve digestive discomfort. Its active compound, menthol, exhibits antispasmodic effects, which help relax the muscles of the digestive tract, alleviate cramping, and reduce intestinal spasms. Peppermint also stimulates bile flow, aids in digestion, and eases symptoms of indigestion, bloating, and irritable bowel syndrome (IBS).

Usage Guidelines for Peppermint:

Preparation: Prepare Peppermint tea by steeping dried Peppermint leaves in hot water for 5-10 minutes.

Dosage: Drink 1-2 cups of Peppermint tea daily between meals or as needed to relieve digestive discomfort.

Application: Sip Peppermint tea slowly to allow its soothing properties to take effect and alleviate gastrointestinal symptoms.

Duration: Use peppermint tea daily routine for digestive issues.

Fennel

Fennel, a flavorful herb with a licorice-like taste, is renowned for its carminative and digestive properties. It contains volatile oils like anethole, which relax the muscles of the digestive tract, reduce gas, bloating, and abdominal cramps, and facilitate smoother digestion. Fennel seeds also stimulate the production of digestive enzymes, promote nutrient absorption, and alleviate symptoms of indigestion, colic, and acid reflux.

Usage Guidelines for Fennel:

Preparation: Chew on a teaspoon of fennel seeds after meals to aid digestion and freshen breath.

Dosage: Consume 1-2 teaspoons of fennel seeds daily or as needed to relieve gastrointestinal discomfort.

Application: Alternatively, brew fennel tea by steeping crushed Fennel seeds in hot water for 5-10 minutes, then strain and drink.

Duration: Incorporate Fennel seeds or tea into your daily routine to maintain optimal digestive health.

Ginger

Ginger, derived from the Zingiber officinale plant, is revered for its potent medicinal properties and widespread use in traditional medicine. It contains bioactive compounds like gingerol and shogaol, which possess anti-inflammatory, antioxidant, and antiemetic effects. Ginger aids digestion by accelerating gastric emptying, relieving nausea, and alleviating symptoms of motion sickness, morning sickness, and gastrointestinal upset.

Usage Guidelines for Ginger:

Preparation: Prepare Ginger tea by steeping fresh Ginger slices or grated Ginger root in hot water for 10-15 minutes.

Dosage: Drink 1-2 cups of Ginger tea daily between meals or as needed to soothe digestive discomfort.

Application: Consume Ginger tea while it's warm to maximize its digestive benefits and alleviate symptoms of indigestion, nausea, or bloating.

Duration: Make Ginger tea a regular part of your daily routine to maintain optimal digestive function and alleviate GI symptoms effectively.

4. Respiratory Diseases

Respiratory diseases affect the lungs, airways, and breathing. These conditions include infections like the common cold, flu, bronchitis, and pneumonia, as well as chronic respiratory disorders such as asthma, chronic obstructive pulmonary disease (COPD), and emphysema. Herbs like Eucalyptus, Mullein, and Thyme have long been used to support respiratory health, alleviate symptoms, and promote clear breathing.

Eucalyptus

Eucalyptus, derived from the leaves of the Eucalyptus tree, contains cineole, a compound with powerful expectorant, decongestant, and antiseptic properties. It helps clear mucus from the airways, reduces inflammation, and relieves respiratory symptoms such as coughing, congestion, and nasal stuffiness. Eucalyptus oil is commonly used in steam inhalations, chest rubs, and aromatherapy to promote easier breathing and relieve respiratory discomfort.

Usage Guidelines for Eucalyptus:

Preparation: Add a few drops of Eucalyptus essential oil to hot water and inhale the steam to open up congested airways and soothe respiratory symptoms.

Dosage: For steam inhalation, use 3-5 drops of Eucalyptus oil in a bowl of hot water, covering your head with a towel and inhaling deeply for 5-10 minutes.

Application: Alternatively, dilute Eucalyptus oil with a carrier oil like coconut or olive oil and apply it to your chest and throat as a chest rub for relief from cough and congestion.

Duration: Perform steam inhalations or apply chest rubs 2-3 times daily or as needed to alleviate respiratory symptoms effectively.

Mullein

Mullein, a flowering plant native to Europe and Asia, has been traditionally used as a respiratory tonic for centuries. Its leaves and flowers contain mucilage, saponins, and flavonoids that exert demulcent, expectorant, and anti-inflammatory effects on the respiratory system. Mullein tea helps soothe irritated mucous membranes, loosen phlegm, and ease coughing associated with bronchitis, asthma, and other respiratory conditions.

Usage Guidelines for Mullein:

Preparation: Prepare Mullein tea by steeping dried Mullein leaves or flowers in hot water for 10-15 minutes.

Dosage: Drink 1-2 cups of Mullein tea daily between meals or as needed to relieve respiratory congestion and cough.

Application: Consume Mullein tea while it's warm to maximize its soothing effects on the respiratory tract and promote the expectoration of mucus.

Duration: Incorporate Mullein tea into your daily routine until respiratory symptoms improve, then continue as needed for ongoing respiratory support.

Thyme

Thyme, an aromatic herb belonging to the mint family, is valued for its antimicrobial, antispasmodic, and expectorant properties. It contains thymol, a potent compound with antibacterial and antifungal effects, making it effective against respiratory infections like bronchitis, sinusitis, and the common cold. Thyme tea helps relieve cough, congestion, and sore throat, making it a popular remedy for respiratory ailments.

Usage Guidelines for Thyme:

Preparation: Brew Thyme tea by steeping fresh or dried Thyme leaves in hot water for 5-10 minutes.

Dosage: Drink 1-2 cups of Thyme tea daily between meals or as needed to alleviate respiratory symptoms.

Application: Sip Thyme tea slowly to soothe throat irritation, reduce coughing, and promote respiratory comfort.

Duration: Use Thyme tea consistently until respiratory symptoms subside, then continue as needed for ongoing respiratory support.

5. Metabolic Disorders

Metabolic disorders often involve abnormalities in insulin function, blood sugar regulation, and lipid metabolism. Herbs like Fenugreek, Cinnamon, and Berberine have been studied for their potential to support metabolic health, improve insulin sensitivity, and regulate blood sugar levels (Sarvesh Sabarathinam, 2022).

Fenugreek

Fenugreek, derived from the seeds of the Trigonella foenum-graecum plant, is rich in soluble fiber and bioactive compounds like saponins and alkaloids. It has been traditionally used to enhance digestion, regulate blood sugar levels, and improve insulin sensitivity. Fenugreek seeds or supplements may help manage diabetes by slowing carbohydrate absorption and enhancing insulin action, leading to better blood glucose control.

Usage Guidelines for Fenugreek:

Preparation: Soak Fenugreek seeds overnight in water, then consume the seeds and water on an empty stomach in the morning.

Dosage: Start with 1-2 teaspoons of soaked Fenugreek seeds per day, gradually increasing to 5-10 grams daily as tolerated for blood sugar control.

Application: Consume Fenugreek seeds with water or incorporate them into meals, soups, or stews for added flavor and health benefits.

Duration: Use Fenugreek seeds regularly as part of a balanced diet and lifestyle to support metabolic health and blood sugar regulation.

Cinnamon

Cinnamon, obtained from the inner bark of the Cinnamomum tree, is prized for its sweet aroma and distinct flavor. It contains bioactive compounds like cinnamaldehyde and cinnamic acid. They all have the ability to improve insulin sensitivity, lower blood sugar levels, and reduce inflammation. Cinnamon supplementation may help enhance glucose metabolism and reduce insulin resistance in individuals with metabolic disorders like type 2 diabetes.

Usage Guidelines for Cinnamon:

Preparation: Sprinkle ground Cinnamon powder on foods and beverages like oatmeal, yogurt, tea, or smoothies for added flavor and health benefits.

Dosage: Aim for 1-2 grams of Cinnamon per day, which is equivalent to about 1/2 to 1 teaspoon of ground Cinnamon powder.

Application: Incorporate Cinnamon into your daily diet by adding it to various dishes, desserts, or beverages to help regulate blood sugar levels.

Duration: Use Cinnamon consistently as part of a balanced diet and lifestyle to support metabolic health and blood sugar control.

Berberine

Berberine is a bioactive compound found in several plants, including Berberis species, goldenseal, and Oregon grape. It has demonstrated significant therapeutic potential for managing metabolic disorders like diabetes, obesity, and dyslipidemia. Berberine works by activating AMP-activated protein kinase (AMPK), which regulates glucose and lipid metabolism, leading to improved insulin sensitivity and reduced blood sugar levels (Sarvesh Sabarathinam, 2022).

Usage Guidelines for Berberine:

Preparation: Take Berberine supplements in capsule or tablet form, preferably with meals to enhance absorption and reduce gastrointestinal side effects.

Dosage: Start with a low dose of 500 mg to 1 gram of Berberine per day, divided into 2-3 doses, and gradually increase to a maximum of 1.5-2 grams per day if needed.

Application: Take Berberine supplements as directed by your healthcare provider, adjusting the dosage based on your response and tolerance.

Duration: Use Berberine supplements consistently under the supervision of a healthcare professional to support metabolic health and blood sugar regulation. Monitor your blood sugar levels regularly and adjust the dosage as needed to achieve optimal results.

6. Renal and Urinary Diseases

Renal and urinary diseases affect the kidneys and urinary system, encompassing conditions like urinary tract infections (UTIs), kidney stones, and chronic kidney disease. Herbs like Cranberry, Dandelion, and Uva Ursi have been traditionally used to support urinary tract health, prevent infections, and promote kidney function (Singh, 2023).

Cranberry

Cranberries, known for their tart flavor and vibrant red color, are rich in antioxidants and compounds like proanthocyanidins, which help prevent bacterial adhesion to the urinary tract walls, reducing the risk of UTIs. Cranberry supplements or juice may be beneficial for individuals prone to recurrent UTIs or those looking to maintain urinary tract health.

Usage Guidelines for Cranberry:

Preparation: Consume unsweetened Cranberry juice or take Cranberry supplements, preferably standardized to contain at least 36 mg of proanthocyanidins per dose.

Dosage: Follow the recommended dosage on the product label, typically ranging from 300 to 500 mg of Cranberry extract or juice concentrate, taken 1-2 times daily.

Application: Drink Cranberry juice or take supplements with plenty of water to help flush out bacteria and support urinary tract health.

Duration: Use Cranberry supplements regularly as a preventive measure or as directed by your healthcare provider to reduce the risk of UTIs and promote urinary tract health.

Dandelion

Dandelion, known for its vibrant yellow flowers and distinctive leaves, has diuretic properties that help increase urine production and promote kidney function. It contains bioactive compounds like flavonoids and sesquiterpene lactones, which have been studied for their potential to support renal health, reduce water retention, and flush out toxins from the body.

Usage Guidelines for Dandelion:

Preparation: Prepare Dandelion tea by steeping dried Dandelion leaves or roots in hot water for 5-10 minutes, then strain and drink the tea.

Dosage: Drink 1-2 cups of Dandelion tea per day or take Dandelion supplements according to the recommended dosage on the product label.

Application: Enjoy Dandelion tea between meals to support kidney function and promote urinary flow. Avoid excessive consumption, especially if you have kidney stones or other renal issues.

Duration: Use Dandelion tea or supplements regularly as part of a balanced diet and lifestyle to support renal health and urinary function.

Uva Ursi

Uva Ursi, also known as bearberry, is a traditional remedy used to treat urinary tract infections and support bladder health. It contains arbutin, a compound that gets converted into hydroquinone in the body, exerting antimicrobial effects against bacteria in the urinary tract. Uva Ursi supplements or tea may help alleviate UTI symptoms and prevent recurrent infections.

Usage Guidelines for Uva Ursi:

Preparation: Brew Uva Ursi tea by steeping dried Uva Ursi leaves in hot water for 10-15 minutes, then strain and drink the tea.

Dosage: Drink 1-2 cups of Uva Ursi tea per day or take Uva Ursi supplements according to the recommended dosage on the product label.

Application: Consume Uva Ursi tea between meals to promote urinary tract health and alleviate UTI symptoms. Avoid prolonged use or high doses, as it may lead to liver damage or other adverse effects.

Duration: Use Uva Ursi tea or supplements for short-term relief of UTI symptoms or as directed by your healthcare provider. Monitor your symptoms and consult a healthcare professional if they persist or worsen.

7. Infectious Diseases

Infectious diseases are caused by pathogenic microorganisms like bacteria, viruses, fungi, or parasites, leading to illnesses ranging from mild infections to severe conditions. Herbs like Echinacea, Goldenseal, and Elderberry have been traditionally used to support the immune system, fight off infections, and alleviate symptoms associated with infectious diseases (Kubala, 2019).

Echinacea

Echinacea, also known as purple coneflower, is renowned for its immune-boosting properties. It contains bioactive compounds like flavonoids, polysaccharides, and alkylamides, which stimulate the immune system's response to infections, reducing the severity and duration of colds, flu, and other respiratory infections (Kubala, 2019).

Usage Guidelines for Echinacea:

Preparation: Take Echinacea supplements in the form of capsules, tablets, or tinctures, following the recommended dosage on the product label.

Dosage: Typically, adults can take 300-500 mg of Echinacea extract or 1-2 ml of tincture 2-3 times daily during the onset of symptoms or as a preventive measure.

Application: Start taking Echinacea supplements at the first sign of infection or during cold and flu season to boost immunity and reduce the risk of respiratory infections.

Duration: Use Echinacea supplements for up to 10 days at a time, then take a break to avoid developing tolerance. Consult a healthcare professional for prolonged or recurrent infections.

Goldenseal

Goldenseal, a perennial herb native to North America, contains berberine, a potent antimicrobial compound that helps fight bacterial and fungal infections. It has been traditionally used to treat respiratory infections, urinary tract infections, and digestive issues, exhibiting broad-spectrum antimicrobial activity. (Kubala, 2019)

Usage Guidelines for Goldenseal:

Preparation: Take Goldenseal supplements in the form of capsules, .tablets, or tinctures, preferably standardized to contain a certain percentage of berberine.

Dosage: Adults can take 500-1000 mg of Goldenseal extract or 2-4 ml of tincture 2-3 times daily for short-term use during infections.

Application: Use Goldenseal supplements as directed on the product label, preferably with meals to enhance absorption and minimize gastrointestinal side effects.

Duration: Limit Goldenseal use to 1-2 weeks for acute infections, and avoid prolonged use due to potential adverse effects. Consult a healthcare professional for guidance on dosage and duration

Elderberry

Elderberry, derived from the berries of the Sambucus nigra plant, is rich in flavonoids like anthocyanins, which possess antiviral properties and help strengthen the immune system's response to infections. Elderberry syrup or supplements can help alleviate symptoms of colds, flu, and viral respiratory infections.

Usage Guidelines for Elderberry:

Preparation: Take Elderberry syrup, capsules, or lozenges according to the recommended dosage on the product label, choosing products made from standardized Elderberry extract.

Dosage: Adults can take 10-15 ml of Elderberry syrup or 300-600 mg of Elderberry extract capsules 2-3 times daily during infections or as a preventive measure.

Application: Start taking Elderberry supplements at the first sign of symptoms or during flu season to boost immunity and reduce the severity of viral infections.

Duration: Use Elderberry supplements for up to 5-7 days to relieve acute symptoms, and consult a healthcare professional for prolonged or recurrent infections.

8. Dermatological Conditions

Dermatological conditions include a wide range of skin disorders, including inflammation, infections, irritations, and wounds. Natural remedies like Aloe Vera, Calendula, and Neem offer therapeutic benefits for treating various dermatological issues, promoting skin healing, and relieving discomfort associated with skin conditions.

Aloe Vera

Aloe Vera, a succulent plant native to arid regions, has been used for centuries for its soothing, moisturizing, and healing properties. Its gel-like substance contains compounds like polysaccharides, vitamins, minerals, and antioxidants, making it effective for alleviating inflammation, promoting wound healing, and soothing skin irritations.

Usage Guidelines for Aloe Vera:

Preparation: Extract the gel from fresh Aloe Vera leaves or use commercially available Aloe Vera gel or creams.

Application: Apply Aloe Vera gel topically to affected areas of the skin, gently massaging it until absorbed. For best results, use Aloe Vera gel 2-3 times daily, especially after cleansing the skin.

Duration: Use Aloe Vera consistently until the skin condition improves, continuing as needed for ongoing maintenance. Discontinue use if any adverse reactions occur and consult a dermatologist if symptoms persist.

Calendula

Calendula, also known as marigold, is a flowering herb renowned for its anti-inflammatory, antimicrobial, and wound-healing properties. It contains flavonoids, triterpenoids, and carotenoids that help reduce inflammation, promote tissue repair, and soothe irritated skin, making it beneficial for various dermatological conditions like eczema, dermatitis, and minor wounds.

Usage Guidelines for Calendula:

Preparation: Use calendula in the form of infused oils, creams, ointments, or tinctures, available at health food stores or pharmacies.

Dosage:

Tea

Adults can Steep 1-2 teaspoons of dried calendula flowers in a cup of boiling water for 10-15 minutes. Drink 2-3 cups per day.

For children (6-12 years), steep 1/2-1 teaspoon and drink 1-2 cups per day.

Tincture

Adults can take 1-2 ml (20-40 drops) of calendula tincture, diluted in a small amount of water, 2-3 times per day. Children (6-12 years) can take 0.5-1 ml (10-20 drops diluted in water, 2-3 times per day.

Capsules

Adults can have 400-800 mg of calendula capsules, taken 1-2 times per day.

Note: Consult a healthcare provider for appropriate dosages based on the child's weight and age.

Creams and Ointments

Apply Calendula cream or ointment to the affected area 2-3 times per day.

Application: Apply Calendula-infused products directly to clean, dry skin, covering the affected area with a thin layer. Reapply Calendula preparations 2-3 times daily or as needed for symptom relief.

Duration: Continue using Calendula until the skin condition improves, monitoring for any signs of irritation or adverse reactions. Consult a healthcare professional if symptoms worsen or persist over time.

Neem

Neem, derived from the leaves and seeds of the Azadirachta indica tree, is revered in traditional Ayurvedic medicine for its potent antibacterial, antifungal, and anti-inflammatory properties. It contains compounds like azadirachtin, nimbin, and nimbidin, which help combat infections, reduce inflammation, and promote skin healing, making it beneficial for conditions like acne, eczema, and psoriasis.

Usage Guidelines for Neem:

Preparation: Use neem oil, creams, lotions, or soaps containing Neem extract, available at health stores or online retailers.

Dosage: Use neem oil for 1-2 times per day. You can use neem cream or ointment for 2-3 times a day. Neem paste can be used for 20-30 minutes before rinsing off.

Application: Apply Neem-infused products directly to clean, dry skin, focusing on affected areas. Use Neem preparations 1-2 times daily, gradually increasing frequency based on tolerance and skin response.

Duration: Use Neem consistently for several weeks to see noticeable improvements in skin condition. Monitor for any adverse reactions like redness, itching, or irritation, and discontinue use if necessary. Consult a dermatologist for personalized recommendations if needed.

9. Reproductive and Gynecological Disorders

Reproductive and gynecological disorders include a range of conditions affecting the female reproductive system, including menstrual irregularities, menopause symptoms, and hormonal imbalances. Natural remedies like Red Raspberry Leaf, Black Cohosh, and Dong Quai offer therapeutic benefits for addressing these issues, promoting reproductive health, and alleviating associated symptoms.

Red Raspberry Leaf

Red Raspberry Leaf, derived from the leaves of the raspberry plant, is valued for its uterine tonic properties and high nutrient content. It contains vitamins, minerals, and antioxidants that support reproductive health, regulate menstrual cycles, and ease menstrual discomfort. Red Raspberry Leaf is commonly used to strengthen the uterus and prepare the body for childbirth.

Usage Guidelines for Red Raspberry Leaf:

Preparation: Prepare Red Raspberry Leaf tea by steeping dried leaves in hot water for 10-15 minutes or using pre-packaged tea bags available at health food stores.

Dosage:

Tea

Adults: Steep 1-2 teaspoons of dried Red Raspberry Leaf in a cup of boiling water for 10-15 minutes. Drink 1-3 cups per day.

Pregnant Women: In the first trimester, start with 1 cup per day. In the second trimester, increase to 2 cups per day. In the third trimester, up to 3 cups per day is generally considered safe.

Children (6-12 years): Steep 1/2-1 teaspoon of dried Red Raspberry Leaf in a cup of boiling water for 10-15 minutes. Drink 1-2 cups per day.

Capsules

Adults: 400-800 mg of Red Raspberry Leaf capsules, taken 1-2 times per day.

Pregnant Women: 400 mg of Red Raspberry Leaf capsules, taken 1-2 times per day.

Children (6-12 years): Consult a healthcare provider for appropriate dosages based on the child's weight and age.

Application: Drink Red Raspberry Leaf tea 1-3 times daily, preferably before meals or between meals. Start with a lower dosage and gradually increase intake as needed for desired effects.

Duration: Use Red Raspberry Leaf consistently throughout the menstrual cycle or as recommended by a healthcare provider. Discontinue use during pregnancy unless advised otherwise by a qualified healthcare professional.

Black Cohosh

Black Cohosh, a perennial herb native to North America, has a long history of use in traditional medicine for managing menopausal symptoms and reproductive health concerns. It contains phytoestrogens and other bioactive compounds that help regulate hormonal balance, reduce hot flashes, and alleviate menstrual discomfort. Black Cohosh is particularly beneficial for women experiencing menopausal symptoms like hot flashes, night sweats, and mood swings.

Usage Guidelines for Black Cohosh:

Preparation: Use standardized Black Cohosh extracts, capsules, or tinctures available at health stores or pharmacies.

Dosage:

Capsules/Tablets

Adults can 20-40 mg of standardized extract, taken 1-2 times per day.

Tea

Adults can take 1 teaspoon of dried root in a cup of boiling water for 10-15 minutes. Drink 1-2 cups per day.

Application: Take Black Cohosh supplements according to the manufacturer's instructions or as directed by a healthcare provider. Start with a low dosage and gradually increase as needed, up to the recommended daily dosage.

Duration: Use Black Cohosh consistently for several weeks to assess its effectiveness in relieving symptoms. Consult a healthcare professional if symptoms persist or worsen over time.

Dong Quai

Dong Quai, also known as Angelica sinensis, is a traditional Chinese herb renowned for its hormone-balancing and menstrual-regulating properties. It contains phytoestrogens, ferulic acid, and other active compounds that help regulate estrogen levels, alleviate menstrual cramps, and promote reproductive health. Dong Quai is commonly used to address menstrual irregularities, premenstrual syndrome (PMS) symptoms, and menopausal discomfort.

Usage Guidelines for Dong Quai:

Preparation: Use Dong Quai in the form of capsules, tinctures, or dried root preparations, available at health food stores or online retailers.

Application: Divide the daily dosage into smaller doses and take them throughout the day with meals.

Dosage:

Capsules/Tablets

500-600 mg taken 1-2 times per day.

Tincture

Take 2-4 ml (40-80 drops), diluted in a small amount of water, 2-3 times per day.

Tea

Take 1-2 teaspoons of root in a cup of boiling water for 10-15 minutes. Drink 1-2 cups per day.

Dried Root

2-4 grams of dried root, taken in divided doses throughout the day.

Duration: Use Dong Quai consistently for several weeks to months to achieve optimal results. Monitor for any adverse reactions or interactions with other medications. Consult a healthcare provider before starting Dong Quai supplementation, especially if pregnant, breastfeeding, or taking prescription medications.

Chapter 7
Healing with Aromatherapy

Aromatherapy becomes a vital practice for you, as it utilizes aromatic plant extracts, commonly known as essential oils, to enhance your physical, emotional, and psychological well-being. Through the utilization of these therapeutic properties, you gain access to a natural and effective means of improving your health and vitality. Here are the five principles of aromatherapy:

Inhalation

The primary method involves inhaling the aroma of essential oils. When you inhale these scent molecules, they travel through your olfactory system to your brain's limbic system, which manages your emotions, memories, and behaviors. This interaction can trigger various physiological responses, such as stress reduction, relaxation promotion, and mood enhancement.

Topical Application

Essential oils can be applied to your skin through massage or topical preparations. When applied topically, the active compounds in essential oils are absorbed into your bloodstream, exerting localized effects on your body. This method is commonly used for pain relief, skin care, and wound healing.

Diffusion

Diffusing essential oils into the air is another popular practice. A diffuser disperses aromatic molecules into the air, allowing you to inhale and absorb them. Diffusion helps purify the air, create a relaxing atmosphere, and support respiratory health.

Combination Therapy

You can combine aromatherapy with other holistic therapies, such as massage, acupuncture, or yoga, to enhance its effectiveness. By integrating aromatherapy into a comprehensive wellness regimen, you can experience synergistic benefits that address both your physical and emotional health.

Individualized Approach

Aromatherapy is highly personalized, and the choice of essential oils depends on your preferences, health concerns, and therapeutic goals. What works for one person may not be suitable for another, so it's essential to tailor aromatherapy treatments to meet your unique needs.

By following these principles, you can effectively harness the healing power of aromatherapy to improve your overall well-being and quality of life. Whether used for relaxation, stress relief, pain management, or immune support, aromatherapy offers a versatile and natural approach to holistic health and healing.

Stress Relief and Mood Enhancement

When it comes to stress relief and mood enhancement, several aromatic herbs prove beneficial. Lavender, chamomile, and rose are among the most notable ones. Lavender, with its calming and soothing properties, can help alleviate stress and promote relaxation. Chamomile is renowned for its gentle sedative effects, making it ideal for easing anxiety and promoting a sense of calm. Rose, with its uplifting and comforting scent, can help uplift your mood and promote emotional well-being (Villines, 2023).

Lavender

Usage Guidelines: Lavender essential oil can be used in aromatherapy diffusers, added to bathwater, or diluted with a carrier oil for massage. For stress relief, add a few drops of lavender oil to your pillow or inhale directly from the bottle.

Importance: Lavender is renowned for its calming and soothing properties. It can help reduce anxiety, promote relaxation, and improve sleep quality. For example, inhaling lavender oil before bedtime can help alleviate stress and induce a sense of calmness, leading to better sleep.

Chamomile

Usage Guidelines: Chamomile essential oil can be diffused, added to bathwater, or diluted with a carrier oil for massage. You can also enjoy chamomile tea for its relaxing effects.

Importance: Chamomile is well-known for its gentle sedative properties, making it effective in reducing anxiety and promoting relaxation. For instance, a warm cup of chamomile tea before bedtime can help calm the mind and prepare you for a restful sleep.

Rose

Usage Guidelines: Rose essential oil can be diffused, added to bathwater, or diluted with a carrier oil for massage. You can also create a rose-scented room spray by mixing rose oil with water in a spray bottle.

Importance: Rose oil has uplifting and comforting properties, making it beneficial for enhancing mood and promoting emotional well-being. For example, inhaling the aroma of rose oil during a stressful day can help uplift your spirits and boost your mood.

Common Aromatic Herbs and Their Uses

In aromatherapy, various aromatic herbs find widespread use due to their therapeutic benefits. Lavender is a versatile herb known for its calming and balancing effects. Peppermint offers invigorating and refreshing properties, making it suitable for alleviating fatigue and enhancing mental clarity. Eucalyptus is prized for its respiratory benefits, helping to clear congestion and support respiratory health. Rosemary is renowned for its stimulating and clarifying effects on the mind, making it useful for improving focus and memory (Shiffler, n.d.). Lemon balm is valued for its calming and uplifting properties, making it ideal for reducing stress and anxiety.

Peppermint

Usage Guidelines: Peppermint essential oil can be diffused to promote alertness and improve focus. It can also be diluted with a carrier oil and applied topically to relieve muscle pain and headaches.

Importance: Peppermint is known for its invigorating and refreshing scent, which helps boost energy levels and mental clarity. For example, inhaling peppermint oil while studying or working can help increase concentration and productivity.

Eucalyptus

Usage Guidelines: Eucalyptus essential oil can be diffused to clear congestion and support respiratory health. It can also be added to steam inhalations or diluted with a carrier oil and applied topically to the chest for cough relief.

Importance: Eucalyptus has powerful decongestant and expectorant properties, making it effective in relieving respiratory symptoms such as coughs and congestion. For example, inhaling eucalyptus oil vapor can help open up the airways and ease breathing during a cold or flu.

Rosemary

Usage Guidelines: Rosemary essential oil can be diffused to improve memory and concentration. It can also be diluted with a carrier oil and massaged onto the scalp to promote hair growth and relieve headaches.

Importance: Rosemary is renowned for its stimulating and clarifying effects on the mind, making it beneficial for enhancing cognitive function and mental clarity. For example, diffusing rosemary oil in the morning can help improve focus and productivity throughout the day.

Lemon Balm

Usage Guidelines: Lemon balm essential oil can be diffused to reduce stress and anxiety. It can also be applied topically to the temples or wrists for its calming effects.

Importance: Lemon balm is valued for its calming and uplifting properties, which help reduce stress, anxiety, and insomnia. For example, inhaling lemon balm oil before a stressful event can help calm nerves and promote a sense of relaxation.

Chapter 8
Boosting Immunity with Herbal Remedies

In this chapter, you will explore how herbal remedies can strengthen your immune system, helping you fend off illnesses and stay healthy. By incorporating these herbs into your routine, you can support your body's natural defenses and enhance your overall well-being.

Before diving into specific herbs, it is important to understand how to boost your immune system effectively. Your immune system works tirelessly to protect you from harmful invaders, and supporting it involves adopting certain lifestyle practices and incorporating immune-boosting herbs into your daily life.

You will discover several herbs renowned for their immune-boosting properties. From traditional remedies to modern supplements, these botanicals offer a natural way to strengthen your body's defenses and protect against infections.

Here's a comprehensive guide on using these herbs effectively:

Power Up Herbs for a Stronger Immune System

Echinacea

Application: Use it as capsules, tinctures, teas, and extracts.

When to Use: Take Echinacea at the first sign of illness or during periods of increased susceptibility to infections, such as during the cold and flu season.

How Long to Use: Use Echinacea for up to 10 days at a time, followed by a break of a few weeks to prevent tolerance.

Preparation: If using Echinacea tea, steep one to two teaspoons of dried Echinacea root or herb in hot water for 10-15 minutes before straining and drinking.

Elderberry

Application: Elderberry is commonly available as syrups, lozenges, teas, and capsules.

When to Use: Take Elderberry preventatively during cold and flu season or at the onset of symptoms to shorten the duration and severity of illness.

How Long to Use: Use Elderberry for up to five days when treating acute symptoms. For preventive purposes, take it daily during times of increased risk.

Preparation: Elderberry syrup can be made by simmering dried elderberries with water and honey until thickened, then straining and storing in a glass jar.

Astragalus

Application: Astragalus is available in various forms, including capsules, tinctures, teas, and powdered extracts.

When to Use: Incorporate Astragalus into your daily routine to support long-term immune health, especially during periods of stress or when exposed to pathogens.

How Long to Use: Take Astragalus regularly for several weeks to months for optimal immune support.

Preparation: To make Astragalus tea, simmer one tablespoon of dried Astragalus root in water for 15-20 minutes, then strain and drink.

By following these usage guidelines, you can harness the immune-boosting properties of Echinacea, Elderberry, and Astragalus to fortify your body's defenses and promote overall well-being. Incorporate these herbs into your wellness routine to stay healthy and resilient year-round.

Herbal Warriors: Defend Your Health Naturally

Garlic

Application: Incorporate raw or cooked garlic into your daily meals. Alternatively, garlic supplements are available in the form of capsules, tablets, and extracts.

When to Use: Consume garlic regularly as part of your diet to support immune function and overall health. You can also increase your intake during cold and flu season or when you feel run down.

How Long to Use: Garlic can be consumed daily as a preventive measure or used for short periods during times of increased susceptibility to illness.

Preparation: To maximize the benefits of raw garlic, crush or chop cloves and let them sit for 10 minutes before consumption to activate its beneficial compounds.

Ginger

Application: Enjoy ginger in various forms, such as fresh ginger root, ginger tea, capsules, or powdered extracts.

When to Use: Incorporate ginger into your daily routine to support digestion, reduce inflammation, and boost immunity. You can also consume it at the onset of cold or flu symptoms.

How Long to Use: Ginger can be consumed regularly as part of your diet or used intermittently for acute conditions. Consult a healthcare professional for long-term use.

Preparation: To make ginger tea, steep fresh ginger slices or grated ginger in hot water for 10-15 minutes, then strain and drink.

Turmeric:

Application: Add ground turmeric to your cooking, or take turmeric supplements available in capsule or powdered form.

When to Use: Use turmeric regularly to reduce inflammation, support joint health, and boost immunity. It can also be beneficial during periods of increased stress or illness.

How Long to Use: Turmeric can be consumed daily as a preventive measure or used for short periods to address specific health concerns.

Preparation: To enhance turmeric absorption, consume it with black pepper or fat-containing foods. You can also make turmeric tea by simmering turmeric powder in milk or water and adding honey or spices for flavor.

Nature's Shield - The Energy and Immunity Booster

Boost your energy and strengthen your immune system with nature's shield - Ginseng, Ashwagandha, and Rhodiola. Here's how you can effectively use these powerful herbs:

Ginseng

Application: Ginseng is available in various forms, including capsules, tablets, extracts, and teas. Choose the form that best suits your preferences and needs.

When to Use: Incorporate ginseng into your daily routine to enhance energy levels, improve focus, and support immune function. It can also be beneficial during times of increased stress or fatigue.

How Long to Use: Ginseng can be used regularly as a tonic herb to promote overall well-being. Follow the recommended dosage instructions provided on the product label or consult a healthcare professional for personalized guidance.

Preparation: If using ginseng tea, steep ginseng slices or powder in hot water for 5-10 minutes, then strain and enjoy.

Ashwagandha

Application: Ashwagandha is commonly available in powdered form, capsules, or liquid extracts. Choose a high-quality ashwagandha supplement from a reputable source.

When to Use: Take ashwagandha regularly to reduce stress, enhance vitality, and support immune function. It can also be useful during periods of physical or mental fatigue.

How Long to Use: Ashwagandha is safe for long-term use, but it's essential to follow recommended dosage guidelines. Consult a healthcare professional for personalized advice.

Preparation: Mix ashwagandha powder into smoothies, juices, or warm milk for a soothing beverage. Alternatively, take capsules or liquid extracts as directed on the product label.

Rhodiola

Application: Rhodiola supplements are available in capsule or tablet form, as well as standardized extracts. Choose a high-quality product with a standardized concentration of active compounds.

When to Use: Take Rhodiola regularly to combat fatigue, increase stamina, and support mental clarity. It can also be beneficial during periods of intense physical or mental exertion.

How Long to Use: Rhodiola can be used continuously for several weeks to months, followed by a break if needed

Preparation: Take Rhodiola supplements with water or a meal to enhance absorption. Avoid taking it late in the day to prevent potential sleep disturbances.

Simple Remedies for Daily Health

Morning Boost Tea

Ingredients: Green Tea, Lemon, Honey, Ginger

How It Helps: Green tea provides antioxidants, lemon boosts vitamin C, honey soothes the throat, and ginger aids digestion. Together, they enhance metabolism, boost immunity, and provide a refreshing start to your day.

Digestive Aid Smoothie

Ingredients: Pineapple, Papaya, Mint Leaves, Ginger

How It Helps: Pineapple and papaya contain digestive enzymes, mint soothes the stomach, and ginger aids digestion and reduces nausea. This smoothie aids in digestion, reduces bloating, and supports gut health.

Energizing Morning Shot

Ingredients: Apple Cider Vinegar, Lemon Juice, Cayenne Pepper

How It Helps: Apple cider vinegar aids digestion, lemon provides vitamin C, and cayenne pepper boosts metabolism. This shot kickstarts your metabolism, aids detoxification, and provides a burst of energy.

Immunity-Boosting Lemon Water

Ingredients: Water, Lemon, Honey, Turmeric

How It Helps: Lemon provides vitamin C, honey soothes the throat, and turmeric boosts immunity with its anti-inflammatory properties. This drink supports overall health, strengthens immunity, and hydrates the body.

Relaxing Chamomile Tea

Ingredients: Chamomile Tea Bag, Honey, Lemon (optional)

How It Helps: Chamomile has calming properties that reduce stress and promote relaxation. Enjoying a cup of chamomile tea before bed helps induce sleep, soothes nerves, and supports restful sleep.

Refreshing Cucumber Mint Water

Ingredients: Cucumber Slices, Mint Leaves, Water

How It Helps: Cucumber hydrates the body, mint aids digestion, and the infusion provides a refreshing drink that promotes hydration, aids digestion, and supports overall well-being.

Ginger Turmeric Golden Milk

Ingredients: Milk (or Plant-Based Milk), Turmeric, Ginger, Honey (optional)

How It Helps: Turmeric and ginger have anti-inflammatory properties, while milk provides calcium and protein. This soothing beverage reduces inflammation, boosts immunity, and supports joint health.

Antioxidant Berry Smoothie

Ingredients: Mixed Berries (Blueberries, Strawberries, Raspberries), Spinach, Almond Milk, Chia Seeds

How It Helps: Berries are rich in antioxidants, spinach provides vitamins and minerals, almond milk adds creaminess and chia seeds offer omega-3 fatty acids. This smoothie supports cellular health, boosts energy, and provides essential nutrients.

Lemon Ginger Detox Water

Ingredients: Water, Lemon, Ginger

How It Helps: Lemon detoxifies the body, ginger aids digestion, and the infusion supports hydration and detoxification. Drinking this water throughout the day helps flush out toxins, aids digestion, and promotes clear skin.

Herbal Immunity Booster Shot

Ingredients: Apple Cider Vinegar, Lemon Juice, Honey, Garlic, Cayenne Pepper

How It Helps: Apple cider vinegar boosts immunity, lemon provides vitamin C, honey soothes the throat, garlic has antimicrobial properties, and cayenne pepper boosts metabolism. This potent shot strengthens the immune system and aids in fighting off infections.

These simple herbal remedies for daily health are easy to incorporate into your routine and offer a natural way to support overall well-being and vitality.

Turmeric Honey Face Mask

Ingredients: Turmeric Powder, Honey, Yogurt (optional)

How It Helps: Turmeric has anti-inflammatory and antibacterial properties, while honey moisturizes and soothes the skin. This face mask helps reduce acne, brightens the complexion, and promotes healthy, glowing skin.

Peppermint Oil Headache Relief

Ingredients: Peppermint Essential Oil, Carrier Oil (such as Coconut Oil)

How It Helps: Peppermint oil's cooling properties reduce headaches and migraines. Apply the diluted oil to the temples and forehead for quick relief from tension headaches.

Rosemary Hair Rinse

Ingredients: Fresh Rosemary Sprigs, Water

How It Helps: Rosemary stimulates hair growth, reduces dandruff, and strengthens hair follicles. Boil rosemary sprigs in water, let it cool, and then use it as a final hair rinse after shampooing to promote healthy hair and scalp.

Soothing Lavender Bath Soak

Ingredients: Epsom Salt, Lavender Essential Oil

How It Helps: Epsom salt relaxes muscles, while lavender essential oil calms the mind and promotes relaxation. Add Epsom salt and a few drops of lavender oil to warm bathwater for a soothing soak that relieves stress and muscle tension.

Herbal Steam Inhalation for Congestion

Ingredients: Eucalyptus Essential Oil, Boiling Water

How It Helps: Eucalyptus oil clears nasal congestion and relieves sinus pressure. Add a few drops of eucalyptus oil to a bowl of boiling water, cover your head with a towel, and inhale the steam to open up the airways and ease breathing.

Sage Throat Gargle

Ingredients: Sage Leaves, Boiling Water, Salt (optional)

How It Helps: Sage has antibacterial properties that help soothe sore throats and reduce inflammation. Steep sage leaves in boiling water, strain, and gargle the warm liquid to relieve throat discomfort and kill bacteria.

Chamomile Eye Compress for Irritated Eyes

Ingredients: Chamomile Tea Bags, Warm Water

How It Helps: Chamomile has anti-inflammatory properties that reduce eye irritation and puffiness. Steep chamomile tea bags in warm water, allow them to cool slightly, then place them over closed eyes for a few minutes to soothe tired or irritated eyes.

Nettle Leaf Hair Rinse

Ingredients: Dried Nettle Leaves, Apple Cider Vinegar, Water

How It Helps: Nettle leaf strengthens hair, reduces shedding, and promotes scalp health. Steep dried nettle leaves in water, strain, add a splash of apple cider vinegar, and use as a final hair rinse to nourish and condition the hair.

Lemon Balm Lip Balm

Ingredients: Lemon Balm Leaves, Coconut Oil, Beeswax

How It Helps: Lemon balm moisturizes and heals chapped lips, while coconut oil and beeswax provide a protective barrier. Infuse lemon balm leaves in coconut oil, strain, and mix with melted beeswax to create a soothing lip balm.

Herbal Foot Soak for Tired Feet

Ingredients: Epsom Salt, Peppermint Essential Oil, Warm Water

How It Helps: Epsom salt relieves muscle soreness, while peppermint oil cools and refreshes tired feet. Dissolve Epsom salt and a few drops of peppermint oil in warm water, soak your feet for 15-20 minutes to relieve fatigue and rejuvenate the feet.

Seasonal Defense with Herbal Strategies All Year-Round

Echinacea Tincture for Immune Support

Description: Echinacea tincture strengthens the immune system and helps prevent colds and flu.

Application: Take 1-2 droppers full of Echinacea tincture daily at the onset of cold symptoms.

When to Use: Start using Echinacea tincture at the beginning of cold and flu season or when exposed to illness.

Duration: Use for up to two weeks at a time, then take a break for one week.

Nettle Leaf Tea for Allergy Relief

Description: Nettle leaf tea reduces allergy symptoms like sneezing and itching by acting as a natural antihistamine.

Application: Steep 1-2 teaspoons of dried nettle leaves in hot water for 5-10 minutes. Drink 2-3 cups daily.

When to Use: Start drinking nettle tea a few weeks before allergy season or when symptoms arise.

How to Prepare: Steep dry nettle leaves in hot water.

Duration: Use throughout allergy season or as needed for symptom relief.

Lemon Balm Salve for Cold Sores

Description: Lemon balm salve soothes and heals cold sores caused by the herpes virus.

Application: Apply the salve directly to cold sores 2-3 times daily until healed.

When to Use: Use at the first sign of a cold sore outbreak.

How to Prepare: Purchase a pre-made lemon balm salve or make your own using lemon balm-infused oil and beeswax.

Duration: Continue use until the cold sore is healed.

Ginger Turmeric Tea for Inflammation

Description: Ginger turmeric tea reduces inflammation and supports overall health.

Application: Boil water and add fresh ginger slices and turmeric powder. Simmer for 10 minutes, then strain and drink.

When to Use: Drink daily for general health or during times of increased inflammation.

How to Prepare: Slice fresh ginger and add to boiling water with turmeric powder.

Duration: Drink daily as needed for inflammation relief.

Chamomile Lavender Pillow Spray for Sleep

Description: Chamomile lavender pillow spray promotes relaxation and better sleep.

Application: Spritz onto pillows and bedding before bedtime.

When to Use: Use nightly to improve sleep quality.

How to Prepare: Mix distilled water with a few drops of chamomile and lavender essential oils in a spray bottle.

Duration: Use at night for ongoing sleep support.

Peppermint Oil Rub for Headaches

Description: Peppermint oil applied to the temples relieves tension headaches and promotes relaxation.

Application: Mix peppermint oil with coconut or almond oil then massage onto the temples.

When to Use: Use as needed at the onset of a headache.

How to Prepare: Dilute peppermint oil with a carrier oil before use.

Duration: Reapply as needed until headache symptoms subside.

Hibiscus Tea for Blood Pressure

Description: Hibiscus tea helps lower blood pressure and promotes heart health.

Application: Steep hibiscus tea bags or dried hibiscus flowers in hot water for 5-10 minutes. Drink 2-3 cups daily.

When to Use: Drink regularly to help manage high blood pressure.

How to Prepare: Steep hibiscus tea bags or dried flowers in hot water.

Duration: Drink daily for ongoing blood pressure support.

Rosehip Seed Oil for Skin Repair

Description: Rosehip seed oil nourishes and repairs the skin, reducing the appearance of scars and wrinkles.

Application: Apply a few drops of rosehip seed oil to clean, damp skin and massage gently until absorbed.

When to Use: Use daily as part of your skincare routine.

How to Prepare: Purchase pre-made rosehip seed oil.

Duration: Use daily for ongoing skin repair and rejuvenation.

Dandelion Root Tea for Liver Support

Description: Dandelion root tea supports liver health and aids digestion.

Application: Steep dandelion root tea bags or dried dandelion root in hot water for 5-10 minutes. Drink 2-3 cups daily.

When to Use: Drink regularly to support liver function, especially after periods of indulgence.

How to Prepare: Steep dandelion root tea bags or dried root in hot water.

Duration: Drink daily for ongoing liver support.

Cayenne Pepper Salve for Joint Pain

Description: Cayenne pepper salve reduces joint pain and inflammation when applied topically.

Application: Apply a small amount of cayenne pepper salve to affected joints and massage gently until absorbed.

When to Use: Use as needed to relieve joint pain.

How to Find: Cayenne pepper salve can be found at health food stores or online, or you can make your own using cayenne pepper powder and a carrier oil.

How to Prepare: Mix cayenne pepper powder with a carrier oil like coconut or olive oil to create a paste.

Seasonal Herbal Recommendations

Spring Renewal with Nettle Tea

Description: Nettle tea helps cleanse the body of winter toxins, boosts energy, and supports seasonal allergies.

Application: Steep dried nettle leaves in hot water for 5-10 minutes. Drink 1-2 cups daily.

When to Use: Drink daily in spring to support detoxification and allergy relief.

How to Prepare: Steep dried nettle leaves in hot water to make tea.

Duration: Drink daily throughout the spring season.

Summer Cooling with Peppermint Infusion

Description: Peppermint infusion cools the body, aids digestion, and provides relief from summer heat.

Application: Steep fresh or dried peppermint leaves in hot water for 5-10 minutes. Drink as desired, hot or cold.

When to Use: Drink throughout the day to stay cool and hydrated during the hot summer months.

How to Prepare: Steep peppermint leaves in hot water to make the infusion.

Duration: Drink as desired throughout the summer season.

Autumn Immune Boost with Elderberry Syrup

Description: Elderberry syrup strengthens the immune system and helps prevent seasonal colds and flu.

Application: Take 1-2 teaspoons of elderberry syrup daily as a preventative measure during cold and flu season.

When to Use: Start taking elderberry syrup in early autumn and continue throughout the season.

How to Prepare: Mix dried elderberries with water and honey, then simmer to make the syrup.

Duration: Take daily throughout the autumn season.

Winter Wellness with Echinacea Tincture

Description: Echinacea tincture boosts the immune system and helps ward off winter illnesses.

Application: Take 1-2 droppers full of echinacea tincture 2-3 times daily at the first sign of a cold or flu.

When to Use: Use as needed during the winter months to prevent and treat colds and flu.

How to Prepare: Echinacea tincture is made by extracting echinacea roots or leaves in alcohol or glycerin.

Duration: Use as needed throughout the winter season.

Year-Round Defense with Garlic Capsules

Description: Garlic capsules support immune function, cardiovascular health, and overall wellness year-round.

Application: Take 1-2 garlic capsules daily with meals.

When to Use: Use consistently throughout the year for ongoing immune support and health benefits.

How to Prepare: Garlic capsules are pre-made and ready to use.

Duration: Take daily for continuous immune support.

Daily Detox: Gentle Herbs for Everyday Cleansing

Liver Love with Milk Thistle Tea

Description: Milk thistle tea supports liver health by aiding in detoxification and promoting overall well-being.

Application: Steep dried milk thistle seeds in hot water for 10-15 minutes. Drink 1-2 cups daily.

When to Use: Enjoy daily as part of a gentle detox regimen or after periods of indulgence.

How to Prepare: Steep dried milk thistle seeds in hot water to make tea.

Duration: Drink regularly for ongoing liver support.

Dandelion Detox Salad

Description: Incorporate fresh dandelion greens into salads to support liver function and aid in detoxification.

Application: Add fresh dandelion greens to salads, sandwiches, or smoothies.

When to Use: Enjoy regularly as part of a healthy diet, especially during detox periods.

How to Find: Dandelion greens can be foraged from pesticide-free areas or purchased at farmers' markets.

How to Prepare: Rinse fresh dandelion greens thoroughly and add them to your favorite dishes.

Duration: Incorporate into meals as desired for ongoing detox support.

Burdock Root Cleansing Soup

Description: Burdock root soup helps cleanse the body by supporting liver and kidney function.

Application: Simmer chopped burdock root with vegetables and herbs to make a nourishing soup.

When to Use: Enjoy regularly as part of a cleansing regimen or to support overall health.

How to Prepare: Peel and chop burdock root, then simmer with other ingredients to make soup.

Duration: Incorporate into your diet as desired for ongoing cleansing benefits.

Quick Fix Herbs for Common Ailments

Ginger Tea for Nausea

Description: Ginger tea is a natural remedy for soothing nausea and upset stomach.

Application: Steep fresh ginger slices in hot water to make tea and sip slowly.

When to Use: Drink at the onset of nausea or when feeling queasy.

How to Prepare: Slice fresh ginger thinly and steep in hot water for 5-10 minutes.

Duration: Drink until symptoms improve.

Chamomile Compress for Eye Irritation

Description: Chamomile has anti-inflammatory properties that can help soothe eye irritation and reduce redness.

Application: Steep chamomile tea bags in hot water, then let them cool before placing them over closed eyes.

When to Use: Use as needed when experiencing eye irritation or inflammation.

How to Prepare: Steep chamomile tea bags in hot water for a few minutes, then let them cool.

Duration: Leave the chamomile compress on closed eyes for 10-15 minutes.

Lemon Balm Salve for Cold Sores

Description: Lemon balm has antiviral properties that can help alleviate cold sores.

Application: Apply lemon balm salve directly to cold sores using a clean cotton swab.

When to Use: Use at the first sign of a cold sore outbreak and continue as needed.

How to Prepare: Make a salve by infusing lemon balm leaves in oil and then mixing with beeswax.

Duration: Apply several times a day until cold sores heal.

Chapter 9
Herbal Care for Children

Herbal remedies can be a gentle and effective way to support the health of children. However, it is important to choose herbs that are safe and appropriate for their age group. This chapter will explore the use of herbs for infants, toddlers, young children, and older children, detailing safe options and usage.

Safe Herbs for Infants

Fennel

Description: Fennel is well-known for its digestive benefits, particularly in relieving colic and gas in infants.

Application: Prepare with 1 teaspoon of fennel seeds in 1 cup of boiling water for 10 minutes. Strain and let it cool.

When to Use: Use fennel tea as needed when your infant is experiencing colic or gas.

How to Find: Fennel seeds are available in grocery stores and health food stores.

How to Prepare: Brew the tea and give 1 teaspoon of the cooled tea to the infant using a dropper or a small spoon.

Duration: Administer up to 3 times a day, as needed.

Chamomile

Description: Chamomile is a calming herb that can help soothe fussy babies and promote better sleep (Sevinç Polat, 2020).

Application: Prepare with 1 teaspoon of dried chamomile flowers in 1 cup of boiling water. Let it steep for 5 minutes, strain, and cool.

When to Use: Use when your infant is fussy, restless, or having trouble sleeping.

How to Find: Dried chamomile flowers or tea bags can be found at grocery stores and health food stores.

How to Prepare: Brew the tea and give 1 teaspoon of the cooled tea to the infant using a dropper or a small spoon.

Duration: Administer up to 2 times a day.

Herbs for Toddlers and Young Children

Catnip

Description: Catnip is a gentle herb that can help calm toddlers and relieve digestive issues.

Application: Prepare using 1 teaspoon of dried catnip in 1 cup of boiling water for 10 minutes. Strain and let it cool.

When to Use: Use as needed to calm an anxious or hyperactive toddler, or to ease digestive discomfort.

How to Find: Dried catnip is available at health food stores.

How to Prepare: Brew the tea and give 1-2 teaspoons of the cooled tea to the child.

Duration: Administer up to 3 times a day.

Lemon Balm

Description: Lemon balm is known for its calming properties and can help reduce anxiety and promote sleep in young children.

Application: Prepare using 1 teaspoon of dried lemon balm in 1 cup of boiling water for 10 minutes. Strain and let it cool.

When to Use: Use when your child is anxious, restless, or having trouble sleeping.

How to Find: Dried lemon balm can be found at health food stores.

How to Prepare: Brew the tea and give 1-2 teaspoons of the cooled tea to the child.

Duration: Administer up to 2 times a day.

Herbs for Older Children

Echinacea

Description: Echinacea is commonly used to boost the immune system and help fight off colds and infections.

Application: Prepare tea by steeping 1 teaspoon of dried echinacea in 1 cup of boiling water for 10 minutes. Strain and let it cool.

When to Use: Use at the onset of cold symptoms or when your child is exposed to illness.

How to Find: Dried echinacea or tea bags are available at health food stores.

How to Prepare: Brew the tea and give 1-2 tablespoons of the cooled tea to the child.

Duration: Administer up to 3 times daily for only one day a week.

Elderberry

Description: Elderberry is rich in antioxidants and vitamins, making it effective for boosting the immune system and combating colds and flu.

Application: Prepare elderberry syrup by simmering 1 cup of dried elderberries with 4 cups of water for 45 minutes. Strain and add honey to taste.

When to Use: Use as a preventative measure during cold and flu season or at the onset of symptoms.

How to Find: Dried elderberries can be found at health food stores, and elderberry syrup is also available pre-made.

How to Prepare: Make the syrup and give 1 teaspoon to the child.

Duration: Administer once daily as a preventative, or up to 3 times a day during illness.

By using these safe and gentle herbal remedies, you can support the health and well-being of the kids naturally. Always start with small doses, monitor for any adverse reactions, and consult with a healthcare professional if you have any concerns.

Chapter 10
Specialized Herbal Protocols

Specialized herbal protocols are targeted approaches using specific herbs to address particular health conditions or enhance certain bodily functions. These protocols involve the careful selection, preparation, and use of herbs to achieve optimal health outcomes. Here, we will explore various protocols for common health concerns, providing detailed usage guidelines for each herb.

Immune System Support

Herbs can play a significant role in supporting and enhancing immune function through various mechanisms. This chapter explores the use of adaptogens, antiviral and antibacterial herbs, and herbs for cold and flu prevention.

Adaptogens for Stress and Immune Balance

Adaptogens are herbs enhance the body's resilience to stressors and support overall health (Chesak, 2022).

Ashwagandha

Description: Ashwagandha is a powerful adaptogen known for its ability to reduce stress and support immune function. (Chesak, 2022).

Application: Ashwagandha can be taken in powder, capsule, or tincture form. For powder, mix 1 teaspoon in warm milk or water once daily. Capsules or tinctures can be taken as per the instructions on the packaging.

When to Use: Use daily to help manage stress and enhance immune function.

How to Grow: Sow seeds in spring, and water sparingly. Harvest roots in late fall.

Rhodiola

Description: Rhodiola helps the body cope with physical and mental stress while boosting immune function. (Chesak, 2022)

Application: Take Rhodiola in capsule or tincture form according to the dosage instructions on the product label.

When to Use: Use during periods of high stress or when feeling fatigued.

How to Grow: Rhodiola grows in well-drained and sandy soil. Plant seeds or cuttings in early spring.

Ginseng

Description: Ginseng is an adaptogen that helps reduce stress and enhances immune response.

Application: Take ginseng as a tea, capsule, or tincture. For tea, steep 1 teaspoon of dried ginseng root in hot water for 10 minutes. Drink once daily.

When to Use: Use daily to support overall health and resilience to stress.

How to Grow: Ginseng prefers shady and rich soil. Plant seeds in the fall and water regularly until established.

Antiviral and Antibacterial Herbs

These herbs have properties that help fight off infections and support the immune system.

Garlic

Description: Garlic has strong antiviral and antibacterial properties that help boost the immune system. (Kubala, 2019).

Application: Consume 1-2 raw garlic cloves daily or take garlic supplements as per the product instructions.

When to Use: Use daily to prevent infections or during an illness.

How to Grow: Garlic is easy to grow in well-drained soil with full sun. Plant cloves in the fall, root side down, about 2 inches deep and 6 inches apart.

Oregano Oil

Description: Oregano oil is a potent antimicrobial that can help fight bacterial and viral infections.

Application: Take oregano oil in capsule form or diluted in water (1-2 drops in a glass of water) once daily.

When to Use: Use during the onset of infection or as a preventative measure.

How to Grow: Oregano prefers full sun and well-drained soil. Plant seeds or cuttings in spring, and water moderately.

Thyme

Description: Thyme has strong antimicrobial properties and can support respiratory health. (Kubala, 2019).

Application: Make tea with one spoon of dried thyme in hot water for 10 minutes. Take 1-2 cups daily.

When to Use: Use during respiratory infections or as a preventative measure.

How to Grow: Grow thyme in a dry and well-drained soil. Sprong is the best season to plant thyme. Water sparingly to thyme.

Herbs for Cold and Flu Prevention

These herbs are particularly effective in preventing and alleviating symptoms of colds and flu.

Ginger

Description: Ginger has anti-inflammatory and antiviral properties, making it effective for cold and flu prevention (Contributors, 2023).

Application: Prepare ginger tea by steeping 1 teaspoon of grated fresh ginger in hot water for 10 minutes. Drink 1-2 cups daily.

When to Use: Use at the first sign of cold symptoms or as a daily preventative.

How to Grow: Ginger prefers partial shade and rich, moist soil. Plant ginger root pieces in spring, water regularly, and harvest the rhizomes in late summer.

Turmeric

Description: Turmeric is known for its anti-inflammatory and immune-boosting properties.

Application: Mix 1 teaspoon of turmeric powder in warm milk or water once daily.

When to Use: Use daily to strengthen the immune system.

How to Grow: Plant rhizomes in spring, water regularly, and harvest in the fall.

Licorice Root

Description: Licorice root has antiviral properties and supports respiratory health.

Application: Prepare tea by steeping 1 teaspoon of dried licorice root in hot water for 10 minutes. Drink 1-2 cups daily.

When to Use: Use during cold and flu symptoms or as a preventative measure.

How to Grow: Licorice prefers full sun and sandy, well-drained soil. Plant seeds or root cuttings in spring, and water regularly.

Using these herbs regularly can help maintain a robust immune system, keeping you healthier throughout the year. Use them as recommended, and remember to rotate herbs to avoid overuse of any single herb.

Detoxification Protocols

Detoxification protocols involve using specific herbs to support and enhance the body's natural detoxification processes. These protocols target various organs and systems to remove toxins and improve overall health. Here, we provide detailed usage guidelines for each herb used in detoxification.

Liver Detox Herbs

The liver plays a crucial role in detoxification. Here are herbs that support liver function and promote detoxification.

Milk Thistle

Description: Milk thistle has the properties best for liver diseases. It helps regenerate liver cells.

Application: Take milk thistle in capsule or tincture form according to the product instructions. For tea, steep 1 teaspoon of crushed milk thistle seeds in hot water for 10 minutes. Drink 1-2 cups daily.

When to Use: Use daily for liver support.

How to Grow: Plan milk thistle in spring in a full sun soil.

Dandelion

Description: Dandelion supports liver function and acts as a mild diuretic.

Application: Make tea using one teaspoon of dried dandelion root in hot water for 10 minutes. Drink 1-2 cups daily.

When to Use: Use daily to support liver health.

How to Grow: Plant seeds in spring.

Burdock Root

Description: Burdock root aids in detoxification and supports liver health.

Application: Prepare a tea by simmering 1 teaspoon of dried burdock root in hot water for 10 minutes. Drink 1-2 cups daily.

When to Use: Use daily to support liver detoxification.

How to Grow: Burdock prefers well-drained soil and full sun. Plant seeds in spring.

Kidney and Urinary Tract Cleansing

Supporting kidney health and cleansing the urinary tract is vital for overall detoxification. Here are herbs that help with kidney and urinary tract health.

Uva Ursi

Description: Uva Ursi helps cleanse the urinary tract and supports kidney health.

Application: Make tea by using one teaspoon of dried uva ursi leaves and boiling for 10 minutes. Drink 1-2 cups daily.

When to Use: Use during urinary tract infections or as a preventative measure.

How to Grow: Uva Ursi grows well in a fully drained soil. Make sure to plant in full sun season. Plant seeds or young plants in spring.

Cranberry

Description: Cranberry helps prevent urinary tract infections by inhibiting bacteria from adhering to the urinary tract walls.

Application: Drink 1-2 cups of unsweetened cranberry juice daily or take cranberry supplements as directed.

When to Use: Use daily for urinary tract health.

How to Grow: Cranberries prefer acidic, well-drained soil and full sun. Plant in spring and maintain a consistent water supply.

Nettle

Description: Nettle supports kidney function and acts as a diuretic.

Application: Prepare tea by steeping 1 teaspoon of dried nettle leaves in hot water for 10 minutes. Drink 1-2 cups daily.

When to Use: Use daily to support kidney health.

How to Grow: Moist, rich soil, and partial shade are best to grow nettle. It is best to sow seeds or cuttings in spring.

Digestive System Cleansing

Maintaining a healthy digestive system is crucial for overall detoxification. Here are herbs that aid digestion and support the cleansing process.

Peppermint

Description: Peppermint soothes the digestive system and alleviates bloating and gas.

Application: Prepare a tea by steeping one spoon of dried peppermint leaves and boil for 10 minutes. Drink 1-2 cups daily.

When to Use: Use after meals or when experiencing digestive discomfort.

How to Grow: Well-drained soil and partial shade are best for peppermint growth. Spring season is the most suitable to plant seeds or cuttings.

Fennel

Description: Fennel aids digestion and reduces bloating and gas.

Application: Prepare a tea by steeping 1 teaspoon of crushed fennel seeds in hot water for 10 minutes. Drink 1-2 cups daily.

When to Use: Use after meals or when experiencing digestive discomfort.

How to Grow: Fennel prefers full sun and well-drained soil. Plant seeds in spring.

Aloe Vera

Description: Aloe Vera soothes the digestive tract and promotes regular bowel movements.

Application: Consume 1-2 tablespoons of aloe vera juice daily.

When to Use: Use daily to support digestive health.

How to Grow: Well-drained sun and full sun are the most suitable conditions for the growth of aloe vera. Plant aloe vera pups in spring.

Skin Detoxification

Detoxifying the skin can help improve its appearance and health. Here are herbs that support skin detoxification and health.

Calendula

Description: Calendula has anti-inflammatory and healing properties that benefit the skin.

Application: Prepare tea by steeping 1 teaspoon of dried calendula flowers in hot water for 10 minutes. Use the tea as a wash for the skin or drink 1-2 cups daily.

When to Use: Use as needed for skin health.

How to Grow: Calendula prefers well-drained soil and full sun. Plant seeds in spring.

Neem

Description: Neem has antibacterial and anti-inflammatory properties that support skin health.

Application: Use neem oil directly on the skin or prepare a tea by steeping 1 teaspoon of dried neem leaves in hot water for 10 minutes. Use the tea as a wash for the skin.

When to Use: Use as needed for skin health.

How to Grow: Neem prefers well-drained soil and full sun. Plant seeds or young plants in spring.

Red Clover

Description: Red clover supports skin health by promoting detoxification.

Application: Prepare tea by steeping 1 teaspoon of dried red clover flowers in hot water for 10 minutes. Drink 1-2 cups daily.

When to Use: Use daily to support skin detoxification.

How to Grow: Red clover prefers well-drained soil and full sun. Plant seeds in spring.

These herbal detoxification protocols can help support various bodily functions and promote overall health. By using these herbs regularly, you can enhance your body's natural detoxification processes and improve your well-being.

Chronic Condition Management

Managing chronic conditions with herbal remedies can offer a natural way to alleviate symptoms and enhance overall well-being. Below, you will find specific herbs for diabetes and blood sugar control, cardiovascular health, and joint and muscle pain.

Herbs for Diabetes and Blood Sugar Control

Managing blood sugar levels is crucial for individuals with diabetes. Here are some effective herbs known for their blood sugar-regulating properties:

Fenugreek

Description: Fenugreek lowers blood sugar levels and improve insulin sensitivity.

Application: Soak 1 teaspoon of fenugreek seeds overnight and consume them in the morning. Alternatively, take fenugreek capsules or drink fenugreek tea made by steeping 1 teaspoon of crushed seeds in hot water for 10 minutes. Drink once daily.

When to Use: Use daily, preferably before meals, to help manage blood sugar levels.

How to Grow: Fenugreek prefers well-drained soil and full sun. Plant seeds in spring or early summer.

Cinnamon

Description: Cinnamon has compounds that improve insulin sensitivity and lower blood sugar levels.

Application: Add 1 teaspoon of ground cinnamon to your tea, smoothies, or oatmeal daily. Alternatively, take cinnamon supplements as directed.

When to Use: Use daily, preferably in the morning, to help stabilize blood sugar levels.

How to Grow: Cinnamon trees require a tropical climate. However, you can grow cinnamon basil or Ceylon cinnamon in a pot indoors.

Bitter Melon

Description: Bitter melon contains compounds that mimic insulin and help regulate blood sugar levels.

Application: Consume bitter melon juice, or cook bitter melon as a vegetable. You can also take bitter melon supplements as directed.

When to Use: Use daily to support blood sugar control.

How to Grow: Bitter melon grows well in warm climates. Plant seeds in a sunny spot with well-drained soil.

Support for Cardiovascular Health

Maintaining heart health is essential for preventing cardiovascular diseases. These herbs are known for their heart-protective properties:

Hawthorn

Description: improves blood circulation and reduces blood pressure.

Application: Take hawthorn berries or leaves in the form of tea, tincture, or capsules. Steep 1 teaspoon of dried hawthorn leaves or berries in hot water for 10 minutes. Drink 1-2 cups daily.

When to Use: Use daily to support heart health.

How to Grow: Use well-drained soil and full sun to grow hawthorn trees. Plant hawthorn seeds or saplings in spring.

Garlic

Description: Garlic has compounds that help reduce blood pressure, cholesterol, and inflammation.

Application: Incorporate raw or cooked garlic into your meals. You can also take garlic supplements as directed.

When to Use: Use daily, preferably with meals, for cardiovascular benefits.

How to Grow: Garlic grows best in well-drained soil with full sun. Plant cloves in autumn.

Ginko biloba

Description: Ginko biloba improves blood circulation and helps protect the heart and blood vessels.

Application: Take ginko biloba supplements or brew ginkgo tea by steeping 1 teaspoon of dried leaves in hot water for 10 minutes. Drink once daily.

When to Use: Use daily to enhance cardiovascular health.

How to Grow: Ginkgo trees prefer well-drained soil and full sun. Plant ginkgo seeds or young plants in spring.

Herbs for Joint and Muscle Pain

Herbs with anti-inflammatory and analgesic properties can help manage joint and muscle pain effectively:

Turmeric

Description: Turmeric contains curcumin, a powerful anti-inflammatory compound that helps reduce pain and swelling.

Application: Add 1 teaspoon of turmeric powder to your smoothies, soups, or teas. Alternatively, take turmeric supplements as directed.

When to Use: Use daily to manage pain and inflammation.

How to Grow: To grow turmeric use well-drained soil and partial shade. Plant rhizomes in spring or early summer.

Willow Bark

Description: Willow bark contains salicin, a compound that has pain-relieving and anti-inflammatory effects similar to aspirin.

Application: Make willow bark tea by steeping 1 teaspoon of dried bark in hot water for 10 minutes. Drink 1-2 cups daily. Alternatively, take willow bark capsules as directed.

When to Use: Use daily or as needed for pain relief.

How to Grow: Willow trees grow best in moist, well-drained soil and full sun. Plant willow cuttings in spring.

Devil's Claw

Description: Devil's claw has anti-inflammatory properties that help reduce pain and improve joint mobility.

Application: Prepare tea by steeping 1 teaspoon of dried devil's claw root in hot water for 10 minutes. Drink 1-2 cups daily. You can also take devil's claw supplements as directed.

When to Use: Use daily to manage joint and muscle pain.

How to Grow: Well-drained soil and full sun are the most suitable conditions to grow devil's claw. Plant seeds or young plants in spring.

These herbs provide natural support for managing chronic conditions. Incorporate them into your daily routine, improve your quality of life, and support your long-term health.

Managing Chronic Fatigue and Fibromyalgia

This section focuses on the use of St. John's Wort, Valerian Root, and Magnesium-rich herbs in managing CFS and FM.

St. John's Wort

Description: It is used primarily for its antidepressant properties. It contains active compounds like hypericin and hyperforin, which help regulate mood and reduce symptoms of depression, anxiety, and stress, often associated with chronic fatigue and fibromyalgia.

Application:

Tea: Steep a teaspoon or two of dried St. John's Wort in a cup of boiling water for 10-15 minutes. Drink two times daily.

Tincture: Take 20-30 drops of St. John's Wort tincture in water or juice up to three times daily.

Capsules: Follow the dosage instructions on the supplement label, typically 300 mg taken three times daily.

When to Use: Use daily, especially during times of heightened stress or depressive episodes. Consistent use over several weeks is recommended for best results.

How to Grow: Sow seeds in early spring and keep the soil consistently moist until germination. Once established, the plant requires minimal care.

Valerian Root

Description: Valerian Root (Valeriana officinalis) is a herb traditionally used to promote sleep and reduce anxiety. It contains compounds like valerenic acid and valepotriates, which have a calming effect on the nervous system, making it beneficial for those experiencing sleep disturbances and anxiety associated with chronic fatigue and fibromyalgia.

Application:

Tea: Steep 1 teaspoon of dried valerian root in a cup of hot water for 10-15 minutes. Drink 30-60 minutes before bedtime.

Tincture: Take 1-2 teaspoons of valerian root tincture in a small amount of water or juice before bedtime.

Capsules: Follow the dosage instructions on the supplement label, typically 300-600 mg taken 30 minutes to two hours before bedtime.

When to Use: Use in the evening or before bedtime to help with sleep and relaxation.

How to Grow: Moist, well-drained soil and partial to full sun are suitable for its growth. Plant seeds or root divisions in early spring. Maintain moist, especially during the growing season.

Magnesium-rich Herbs

Description: Magnesium is a crucial mineral involved in muscle function, nerve transmission, and energy production. Deficiencies in magnesium are common in individuals with chronic fatigue and fibromyalgia, leading to muscle pain, cramps, and fatigue. Incorporating magnesium-rich herbs into the diet can help alleviate these symptoms.

Examples of Magnesium-rich Herbs:

Nettle (Urtica dioica): High in magnesium, nettle can be used to make tea or added to soups and stews.

Dandelion (Taraxacum officinale): Contains significant amounts of magnesium, and its leaves can be used in salads or teas.

Alfalfa (Medicago sativa): Another good source of magnesium, often taken as a tea or in supplement form.

Application:

Nettle Tea: Steep 1 teaspoon of dried nettle leaves in a cup of hot water for 10-15 minutes. Drink 1-2 cups daily.

Dandelion Salad: Add fresh dandelion leaves to salads or smoothies.

Alfalfa Tea: Steep 1 teaspoon of dried alfalfa leaves in hot water for 10-15 minutes. Drink once daily.

When to Use: Use daily as part of a balanced diet to help maintain adequate magnesium levels and support overall health.

How to Grow:

Nettle: Grows in moist, rich soil and partial shade. Plant in early spring.

Dandelion: Can grow in any soil type. Plant in early spring.

Alfalfa: Needs full sun and a well-drained soil. Plant it in spring or early summer.

You can manage symptoms of chronic fatigue and fibromyalgia naturally by the mentioned herbs. Regular use of St. John's Wort and Valerian Root can improve mood and sleep, while magnesium-rich herbs support muscle and nerve function.

Herbs for Autoimmune Conditions

Autoimmune conditions can be debilitating and challenging to manage. However, certain herbs like Boswellia, Cat's Claw, and Turmeric have shown promise in supporting immune function and reducing inflammation associated with autoimmune disorders (Hafsa, 2023),

Boswellia

Description: Boswellia (Boswellia serrata), also known as Indian frankincense, is renowned for its potent anti-inflammatory properties. It contains boswellic acid, which inhibits inflammatory pathways and can help manage symptoms of autoimmune conditions such as rheumatoid arthritis and inflammatory bowel disease. (Hafsa, 2023).

Application:

Capsules: Take 300-500 mg of Boswellia extract standardized to 30-60% boswellic acid, 2-3 times daily.

Tincture: Take 20-30 drops of Boswellia tincture in water or juice, 2-3 times daily.

Topical Application: Use Boswellia cream on affected joints or muscles as needed.

When to Use: Use daily to help manage chronic inflammation. Consistent use over several weeks is recommended for best results.

How to Grow: Boswellia trees prefer dry, well-drained soil and full sun. They are best suited for arid climates. Plant seeds or saplings in the spring and water sparingly.

Cat's Claw

Description: Cat's Claw (Uncaria tomentosa) is a vine native to the Amazon rainforest. It has been traditionally used for its immune-boosting and anti-inflammatory properties, making it beneficial for autoimmune conditions like lupus and multiple sclerosis. (Hafsa, 2023).

Application:

Tea: Steep 1 teaspoon of dried Cat's Claw bark in a cup of hot water for 10-15 minutes. Drink 1-2 cups daily.

Capsules: Take 20-60 mg of standardized Cat's Claw extract, 1-2 times daily.

Tincture: Take 20-30 drops of Cat's Claw tincture in water or juice, 2-3 times daily.

When to Use: Use daily to support the immune system and reduce inflammation.

How to Grow: Cat's Claw thrives in well-drained soil and partial to full sun. It is a tropical plant, so it is best grown in warm, humid environments. Plant seeds or cuttings in the spring.

Turmeric

Description: Turmeric (Curcuma longa) is a vibrant yellow spice commonly used in Indian cuisine. It contains curcumin, a powerful anti-inflammatory compound that has been extensively studied for its benefits in managing autoimmune conditions such as rheumatoid arthritis and inflammatory bowel disease.

Application:

Tea: Boil 1 teaspoon of turmeric powder in a cup of water for 10 minutes. Add honey or lemon to taste. Drink 1-2 cups daily.

Capsules: Take 500 mg of curcumin extract, 2-3 times daily.

Golden Milk: Mix 1 teaspoon of turmeric powder with warm milk (or a milk alternative) and a pinch of black pepper. Drink once daily.

When to Use: Use daily to reduce inflammation and support immune function. For best results, combine with black pepper to enhance absorption.

How to Grow: Turmeric prefers warm, humid conditions and well-drained, fertile soil. Plant rhizomes in the spring and keep the soil consistently moist.

Part IV
THE GUIDELINES AND PRECAUTIONS

Chapter 11
Setting Up Your Home Apothecary

Creating a home apothecary is an enriching and practical way to harness the healing power of herbs. By having a dedicated space for your herbal remedies, you can easily access natural treatments for common ailments, support overall wellness, and develop a deeper connection with the natural world. This chapter will guide you through the essentials of setting up your home apothecary, including the tools you need, how to store herbs, and essential herbs to have on hand.

Essentials for Your Home Apothecary

Tools and Equipment

Herb Storage Containers: Glass jars with airtight lids are ideal for storing dried herbs. They keep the herbs fresh and protect them from light, air, and moisture.

Mortar and Pestle: Useful for grinding herbs into powders or pastes.

Herb Grinder: A small electric grinder can save time when processing large quantities of dried herbs.

Tea Infuser: For making herbal teas, a metal or silicone infuser works well.

Measuring Spoons and Cups: Accurate measurements are important when preparing herbal remedies.

Dropper Bottles: Essential for storing tinctures and liquid extracts.

Cheesecloth or Muslin Bags: Useful for straining infusions and decoctions.

Scale: A small kitchen scale helps in accurately measuring herbs by weight.

Labels and Markers: Clearly label all your herbs and preparations with the name and date.

Storing Herbs

Proper storage is crucial to maintaining the potency and efficacy of your herbs. Here are some guidelines:

Dry Herbs Thoroughly: Ensure that herbs are completely dry before storing them to prevent mold and degradation.

Airtight Containers: Use glass jars with tight-fitting lids to keep out air and moisture.

Cool, Dark Place: Store herbs in a cool, dark place to protect them from light and heat, which can degrade their potency.

Label Everything: Always label your jars with the name of the herb and the date it was harvested or stored.

Essential Herbs for Your Home Apothecary

Here is a list of essential herbs that cover a wide range of common ailments and health needs:

Chamomile: For calming, sleep, and digestive issues.

Lavender: For stress relief, sleep, and skin conditions.

Peppermint: For digestive issues, headaches, and respiratory health.

Echinacea: For immune support and cold prevention.

Ginger: For nausea, digestion, and inflammation.

Turmeric: For inflammation, joint health, and digestive health.

Garlic: For immune support and cardiovascular health.

Calendula: For skin health and wound healing.

Dandelion: For liver health and detoxification.

Thyme: For respiratory health and digestive issues.

Elderberry: For immune support and cold prevention.

Rosemary: For memory, digestion, and hair health.

Sage: For throat health, memory, and digestion.

Lemon Balm: For anxiety, sleep, and digestion.

St. John's Wort: For mood regulation and nerve pain.

How to Prepare and Use Your Herbs

Herbal Teas and Infusions

Infusions are a simple and effective way to extract the medicinal properties of herbs, especially leaves and flowers. Here is a basic method for making herbal infusions:

Ingredients: 1-2 teaspoons of dried herb per cup of water.

Method: Boil water, pour over the herbs, cover, and steep for 10-15 minutes. Strain and drink.

When to Use: Infusions can be consumed daily as part of your wellness routine or when needed to address specific ailments.

Decoctions

Decoctions are used for extracting the medicinal properties of tougher plant materials, such as roots, bark, and seeds.

Ingredients: 1-2 tablespoons of dried herb per cup of water.

Method: Place herbs in a pot with water, bring to a boil, then simmer for 20-30 minutes. Strain and drink.

When to Use: Use decoctions for deeper, more chronic conditions and consume as needed.

Tinctures

Tinctures are concentrated liquid extracts made using alcohol or glycerin.

Ingredients: Fresh or dried herbs and a high-proof alcohol (vodka or brandy) or glycerin.

Method: Fill a jar with herbs, cover with alcohol or glycerin, seal, and store in a cool, dark place for 4-6 weeks, shaking occasionally. Strain and bottle.

When to Use: Tinctures are potent and should be used in small doses, typically 20-30 drops in water or juice, 2-3 times daily.

Salves and Balms

Salves are topical preparations used for skin conditions and wounds.

Ingredients: Herbal oil (infused with healing herbs), beeswax.

Method: Melt beeswax, add herbal oil, mix well, and pour into containers to set.

When to Use: Apply salves to affected areas as needed for skin healing and relief.

Herbal Oils

Herbal oils are used for massage, skincare, and healing.

Ingredients: Fresh or dried herbs and a carrier oil (such as olive, coconut, or almond oil).

Method: Place herbs in a jar, cover with oil, seal, and let sit in a sunny spot for 2-4 weeks, shaking occasionally. Strain and bottle.

When to Use: Use herbal oils for massages, skin hydration, and topical healing.

Growing Your Own Herbs

Starting your own herb garden can be a rewarding and practical way to ensure a fresh supply of medicinal plants. Here are some tips for growing a few essential herbs:

Chamomile

How to Grow: Requires a soil in a sunny location. Must water on regular basis but do not overwater. Harvest flowers when they are fully open.

Use: Make teas and infusions for calming effects and digestive health.

Lavender

How to Grow: Prefers to grow in a well-drained soil in full sun. Lavender prefers dry conditions, so water sparingly. Harvest flowers just before they fully open.

Use: Use for stress relief, sleep, and skin health.

Peppermint

How to Grow: Plant in moist, well-drained soil in partial to full sun. Peppermint spreads quickly, so consider growing in containers. Harvest leaves as needed.

Use: Use for digestive issues, headaches, and respiratory health.

Echinacea

How to Grow: Plant in well-drained soil in full sun. Echinacea is drought-tolerant once established. Harvest roots in the fall and leaves and flowers during the growing season.

Use: Use for immune support and cold prevention.

Ginger

How to Grow: Plant ginger rhizomes in rich, well-drained soil in a warm, humid environment. Keep soil moist and harvest rhizomes after 8-10 months.

Use: Use for nausea, digestion, and inflammation.

Understanding Herbal Properties

Understanding the properties of herbs is essential for effectively using them in herbal medicine. This involves knowledge of the active compounds in herbs, how these compounds interact with the body, and the importance of quality and sourcing.

Active Compounds in Herbs

Active compounds are the chemical constituents in herbs responsible for their therapeutic effects. These compounds can include alkaloids, flavonoids, tannins, glycosides, terpenoids, saponins, and essential oils. Here are some examples:

Alkaloids

Example: Berberine (found in Goldenseal)

Effects: Antimicrobial, anti-inflammatory, and blood sugar regulation

Flavonoids

Example: Quercetin (found in Elderberry)

Effects: Antioxidant, anti-inflammatory, and immune-boosting

Tannins

Example: Tannic acid (found in Witch Hazel)

Effects: Astringent, antimicrobial, and anti-inflammatory

Glycosides

Example: Salicin (found in Willow Bark)

Effects: Pain relief and anti-inflammatory

Terpenoids

Example: Thymol (found in Thyme)

Effects: Antimicrobial, antifungal, and antiseptic

Saponins

Example: Ginsenosides (found in Ginseng)

Effects: Immune modulation, anti-inflammatory, and adaptogenic

Essential Oils

Example: Menthol (found in Peppermint)

Effects: Analgesic, cooling, and digestive aid

Understanding these compounds helps in choosing the right herbs for specific health conditions.

How Herbs Interact with the Body

Herbs interact with the body in various ways, influencing physiological processes to promote health and healing. Here are some key mechanisms:

Modulating Immune Response

Herbs: Echinacea, Astragalus

Mechanism: Stimulate immune cells and increase the production of antibodies

Anti-inflammatory Action

Herbs: Turmeric, Ginger

Mechanism: The mechanism of these herbs is simple. The stay in the inflammatory pathways and reduce the production of pro-inflammatory cytokines

Antioxidant Activity

Herbs: Green Tea, Elderberry

Mechanism: Neutralize free radicals and reduce oxidative stress

Antimicrobial Effects

Herbs: Garlic, Oregano

Mechanism: Inhibit the growth of bacteria, viruses, and fungi

Hormonal Balance

Herbs: Chasteberry, Black Cohosh

Mechanism: Influence the production and regulation of hormones

Nervous System Support

Herbs: St. John's Wort, Valerian

Mechanism: Modulate neurotransmitter levels and support nervous system function

Digestive Support

Herbs: Peppermint, Fennel

Mechanism: Enhance digestive enzyme activity and soothe the gastrointestinal tract

Understanding how herbs work in the body helps in selecting the right herbs for specific therapeutic purposes and combining them effectively.

The Importance of Quality and Sourcing

The efficacy and safety of herbal remedies are significantly influenced by the quality of the herbs used. Poor-quality herbs may lack potency and can even be harmful. Here are important considerations:

Quality

Potency: High-quality herbs have higher concentrations of active compounds.

Purity: Herbs should be free from contaminants such as pesticides, heavy metals, and adulterants.

Freshness: Freshly harvested herbs or well-preserved dried herbs retain more of their active compounds.

Sourcing

Organic: Organic herbs are grown without synthetic pesticides and fertilizers, reducing the risk of contamination.

Sustainable: Herbs sourced sustainably help protect natural ecosystems and ensure the longevity of plant species.

Local: Locally sourced herbs may be fresher and support local economies.

Tips for Ensuring Quality

Buy from Reputable Suppliers, choose suppliers with good reputations for quality and ethical sourcing.

Check for Certifications, and look for certifications like USDA Organic, Fair Trade, and Non-GMO.

Inspect the Product. High-quality dried herbs should have vibrant colors and strong aromas.

Understanding the properties of herbs, including their active compounds and how they interact with the body, is crucial for effective herbal medicine use. Ensuring the quality and proper sourcing of herbs maximizes their therapeutic potential and safety. By integrating this knowledge into your practice, you can make informed decisions about which herbs to use to support health and wellness.

Dosage and Administration

Understanding the proper dosage and administration of herbal remedies is crucial for ensuring their effectiveness and safety. This section will provide general dosage guidelines for different forms of herbal remedies, age-specific dosage recommendations, and methods of administration.

General Dosage Guidelines for Different Forms

Herbs can be prepared and consumed in various forms, including teas, tinctures, and capsules. Each form has its specific dosage guidelines:

Teas

Preparation: Steep 1-2 teaspoons of dried herb in a cup of hot water for 5-10 minutes.

Dosage: Drink 1-3 cups per day, depending on the herb and condition.

Examples: Chamomile for calming effects and peppermint for digestion.

Tinctures

Preparation: Tinctures are concentrated liquid extracts made by soaking herbs in alcohol or glycerin.

Dosage: Typically, 1-3 ml (20-60 drops) diluted in water, taken 1-3 times per day.

Examples: Echinacea for immune support and valerian for sleep.

Capsules

Preparation: Capsules contain powdered or encapsulated herbal extracts.

Dosage: Usually, 1-2 capsules (500-1000 mg) taken 1-3 times per day.

Examples: Turmeric for inflammation and garlic for heart health.

Age-specific Dosage Recommendations

Herbal dosages can vary significantly based on age. Children, adults, and the elderly may require different dosages:

Infants and Toddlers (0-2 years)

General Rule: Use only mild herbs and at reduced doses.

Examples:

Chamomile Tea: 1-2 oz of diluted tea, 1-2 times a day.

Fennel Tea: 1-2 oz of diluted tea, 1-2 times a day.

Young Children (2-12 years)

General Rule: Use one-third to one-half of the adult dosage.

Examples:

Echinacea Tincture: 5-10 drops diluted in water, 1-2 times a day.

Lemon Balm Tea: Half a cup, 1-2 times a day.

Adolescents (12-18 years)

General Rule: Use two-thirds of the adult dosage.

Examples:

Peppermint Capsules: 250-500 mg, 1-2 times a day.

Elderberry Syrup: 1 teaspoon, 2-3 times a day.

Adults (18-65 years)

General Rule: Use standard adult dosages.

Examples:

Ginger Tea: 1 cup, 2-3 times a day.

Garlic Capsules: 500-1000 mg, 1-2 times a day.

Elderly (65+ years)

General Rule: Use half to two-thirds of the adult dosage, depending on the individual's health and tolerance.

Examples:

Ginko biloba Tincture: 10-20 drops diluted in water, use twice daily.

Turmeric Capsules: Up to two times a day take a 250-500 mg capsule..

Methods of Administration

Herbs can be administered through various methods depending on the condition and desired effect:

Topical

Application: Apply herbal preparations directly to the skin.

Examples:

Aloe Vera Gel: Apply to burns and skin irritations as needed.

Arnica Cream: Apply to bruises and muscle pain 2-3 times a day.

Oral

Application: Consume herbs by mouth in the form of teas, tinctures, capsules, or syrups.

Examples:

Chamomile Tea: Drink 1-3 times a day for calming effects.

Echinacea Tincture: Take 1-3 ml diluted in water, 1-3 times a day for immune support.

Inhalation

Application: Breathe in the vapors of essential oils or steam-infused herbs.

Examples:

Eucalyptus Oil: Add a few drops to a bowl of hot water and inhale the steam for respiratory relief.

Peppermint Oil: Use in a diffuser to clear nasal congestion and invigorate the senses.

Proper dosage and administration of herbal remedies are essential for their effectiveness and safety. By following general dosage guidelines for different forms, adjusting doses based on age, and using appropriate methods of administration, you can maximize the benefits of herbs while minimizing potential risks. Always start with lower doses and gradually increase as needed, paying close attention to your body's response.

Consulting with Healthcare Professionals

The world of herbal remedies can be complex, and it is essential to seek guidance from healthcare professionals to ensure safe and effective use. This section covers the role of herbalists and integrative medicine practitioners when to consult a professional, and considerations when combining herbal remedies with conventional treatments.

The Role of Herbalists and Integrative Medicine Practitioners

Herbalists are professionals trained in the use of plants for medicinal purposes. They possess in-depth knowledge of herbs, their properties, and how they interact with the body. Herbalists can provide personalized recommendations based on individual health conditions and preferences.

Integrative medicine practitioners combine conventional medical treatments with complementary and alternative therapies, such as herbal medicine, acupuncture, and dietary supplements. They take a holistic approach to healthcare, considering the physical, emotional, and spiritual aspects of well-being.

When to Consult a Professional

While herbs offer numerous health benefits, consulting with a healthcare professional is advisable under certain circumstances:

Chronic or Serious Conditions

If you have a chronic or serious health condition, consult with a healthcare provider is mandatory before you proceed with the herbal remedies. They will guide you on the safety and appropriateness of specific herbs for your condition.

Pregnancy and Breastfeeding

Pregnant or breastfeeding women should seek professional advice before using herbal remedies, as some herbs may pose risks to the developing fetus or nursing infant.

Interaction with Medications

Certain herbs may interact with prescription medications, potentially altering their effectiveness or causing adverse effects. If you're taking medications, consult with a healthcare professional before adding herbal remedies to your regimen.

Combining Herbal Remedies with Conventional Treatments

Integrating herbal remedies with conventional medical treatments requires careful consideration and coordination:

Monitor Effects and Adjustments

Pay close attention to how your body responds to the combined treatment approach. Report any changes or adverse effects to your healthcare providers, who can make adjustments as needed to optimize your health outcomes.

Chapter 12
Precautionary Measures

When using herbal remedies, it is essential to observe precautionary measures to ensure safe and effective outcomes. This section highlights key precautions to consider before and during the use of herbal remedies.

Research and Education

Thorough Research

Before using any herbal remedy, conduct thorough research to understand its properties, potential side effects, and interactions with medications or existing health conditions. Reliable sources such as reputable books, peer-reviewed journals, and trustworthy websites can provide valuable information.

Educate Yourself

Take the time to educate yourself about herbal medicine principles, dosage guidelines, and proper administration methods. Being well-informed empowers you to make informed decisions regarding your health and wellness.

Consultation with Healthcare Professionals

Healthcare Provider Consultation

Always consult with a qualified healthcare professional, such as a physician, herbalist, or naturopathic doctor, before starting any herbal remedy regimen, especially if you have underlying health concerns or are taking medications.

Disclose Medical History

Provide your healthcare provider with a comprehensive medical history, including any existing health conditions, allergies, medications, or supplements you are currently taking. This information will help them assess the safety and suitability of herbal remedies for your individual needs.

Quality and Safety

Avoid Contaminated or Adulterated Products

Be cautious of herbal products that may be contaminated with pesticides, heavy metals, or other harmful substances. Choose organic or wildcrafted herbs whenever possible to minimize exposure to potentially harmful chemicals.

Start Slowly and Monitor the Effects

Start with Low Dosages

Begin with low dosages of herbal remedies, especially if you are new to using them. Gradually increase the dosage if required, but only do it with complete monitoring of your body and any adverse reactions.

Monitor for Adverse Reactions

Pay attention to any adverse reactions or side effects that may occur after taking herbal remedies. These may include allergic reactions, digestive discomfort, headaches, or changes in mood or energy levels. Discontinue use and seek medical attention if adverse reactions persist or worsen.

Pregnancy and Pediatric Considerations

Pregnancy and Lactation

Exercise caution when using herbal remedies during pregnancy or breastfeeding, as certain herbs may pose risks to the developing fetus or nursing infant. Consult with a qualified healthcare provider before using any herbal products during these periods.

Pediatric Use

Use extra caution when administering herbal remedies to infants, children, or adolescents. Certain herbs may not be suitable for pediatric use or may require dosage adjustments based on age and weight. Consult with a pediatrician or healthcare provider experienced in pediatric herbal medicine for guidance.

Storage and Disposal

Proper Storage

Store herbal remedies in a cool, dry place away from direct sunlight and moisture to maintain their potency and shelf life. Follow the storage instructions provided on product labels to ensure optimal effectiveness.

Disposal of Expired Products

Safely dispose of expired or unused herbal products according to local regulations and guidelines. Avoid flushing herbal remedies down the drain or disposing of them in household trash to prevent environmental contamination.

By adhering to these precautionary measures, you can enhance the safety and effectiveness of your herbal remedy use while minimizing potential risks and maximizing health benefits. Remember that individual responses to herbal remedies may vary, so it is essential to approach their use with care and vigilance.

Allergies and Sensitivities

Using herbal remedies for a wellness routine can offer numerous health benefits, but it's crucial to be aware of potential allergies and sensitivities. This section outlines key considerations for identifying, testing, and managing herbal allergies and sensitivities.

Identifying Common Herbal Allergens

Common Culprits

Some herbs are more likely to trigger allergic reactions or sensitivities than others. Common herbal allergens include chamomile, echinacea, feverfew, and members of the Asteraceae family, such as ragweed and daisies. If you have known allergies to certain plants or botanicals, exercise caution when using herbal remedies containing similar ingredients.

Cross-Reactivity

Individuals with pollen allergies may experience cross-reactivity with certain herbal remedies. For example, individuals allergic to ragweed may also react to chamomile or echinacea due to similar protein structures. Be mindful of potential cross-reactivity when selecting herbal products.

Conducting Patch Tests for Topical Herbs

Patch Testing

Before applying herbal preparations to larger areas of your skin, perform a patch test to assess for potential allergic reactions or sensitivities. Wait for 24 to 48 hours after applying to the inner skin. Monitor the test site for any signs of redness, itching, swelling, or rash. If you experience any adverse reactions, discontinue use.

Topical Sensitivities

Some individuals may be more prone to skin sensitivities or contact dermatitis when using herbal remedies topically. If you have sensitive skin or a history of skin reactions, dilute herbal extracts or essential oils with a carrier oil, such as coconut oil or jojoba oil, before applying them to your skin. This can help reduce the risk of irritation while still allowing you to benefit from the herbal properties.

Managing and Treating Herbal Allergies

Symptom Management

If you experience allergic reactions or sensitivities to herbal remedies, promptly discontinue the use of the product and wash the affected area with mild soap and water. Apply a soothing, hypoallergenic cream or ointment to alleviate discomfort and reduce inflammation. Over-the-counter antihistamines or corticosteroid creams may also provide relief from itching and swelling.

Seek Medical Attention

In severe cases of herbal allergies or anaphylaxis, seek immediate medical attention. Allergic reactions can range from mild to life-threatening, so it's essential to monitor symptoms closely and act quickly if symptoms worsen or persist.

Alternative Formulations

If you are allergic to a specific herb or botanical, explore alternative formulations or herbal remedies that do not contain the allergen. Consult with a qualified herbalist or healthcare provider for personalized recommendations tailored to your specific allergies and health needs.

Understanding Herb-Drug Interactions

Mechanisms of Interaction: Herb-drug interactions can occur through various mechanisms, including alterations in drug metabolism, interference with drug absorption, and additive pharmacological effects. Some herbs may affect the activity of liver enzymes responsible for metabolizing medications, leading to changes in drug concentrations in the body.

Individual Variability

The likelihood and severity of herb-drug interactions can vary depending on individual factors such as genetics, underlying health conditions, and medication dosages. Older adults and individuals with compromised liver or kidney function may be at increased risk of experiencing interactions.

Monitoring and Adjusting Dosages

Before you start a herbal supplement, discuss your medication regimen with your healthcare provider to identify potential interactions and determine the safest approach.

Monitor Symptoms

Be vigilant for any changes in symptoms or side effects when starting a new herbal supplement or adjusting medication dosages. If you experience unusual symptoms or adverse reactions, notify your healthcare provider promptly. They can help assess whether the symptoms are related to herb-drug interactions and recommend appropriate management strategies.

Adjusting Dosages

In some cases, it may be necessary to adjust medication dosages when using certain herbs to minimize the risk of interactions. Your healthcare provider can help determine the optimal dosing schedule and monitor your response to treatment over time.

By staying informed about common herbs that interact with medications, understanding the mechanisms of herb-drug interactions, and collaborating with your healthcare provider to monitor and adjust dosages as needed, you can avoid the complexities of herb-drug interactions safely and effectively. Always prioritize open communication with your healthcare team to ensure the best possible outcomes for your health

Safe Use for Different Age Groups

Ensuring the safe use of herbal remedies involves considering the unique needs and vulnerabilities of different age groups. This section provides guidelines for the safe use of herbs across various life stages, including infants and children, adolescents and adults, and considerations for elderly and pregnant women.

Herbs Safe for Infants and Children

Chamomile (Matricaria chamomilla)

Description: Chamomile is a gentle herb known with the properties to calm down and mild flavor. It is often used to soothe fussiness, relaxation, and aid digestion in infants and children.

Dosage: For infants under 6 months, chamomile tea can be diluted and offered in small amounts (1-2 teaspoons). For older children, a weaker tea can be prepared and given in doses of 1-2 tablespoons.

How to Administer: Chamomile tea can be administered to infants using a dropper or spoon. For older children, it can be served warm or cooled in a cup.

When to Use: Chamomile can be used when infants or children are experiencing colic, teething discomfort, or difficulty sleeping. It's also helpful for calming nerves before bedtime.

Catnip (Nepeta cataria)

Description: Catnip is a gentle herb that can induce relaxation and soothe digestive issues in infants and children. It has a mild flavor and is safe for most children.

Dosage: For infants under 6 months, catnip tea can be prepared in small amounts (1-2 teaspoons). For older children, 1-2 tablespoons of a weaker tea can be given.

How to Administer: Catnip tea can be administered to infants using a dropper or spoon. For older children, it can be served warm or cooled in a cup.

When to Use: Catnip is beneficial for infants and children experiencing digestive discomfort, gas, or restlessness. It can also help calm hyperactivity and promote relaxation.

Fennel (Foeniculum vulgare)

Description: Fennel is commonly used to relieve colic, gas, and digestive issues in infants and children. It has a sweet, licorice-like flavor that is generally well-tolerated.

Dosage: For infants under 6 months, fennel tea can be prepared in small amounts (1-2 teaspoons). For older children, a weaker tea can be given in doses of 1-2 tablespoons.

How to Administer: Fennel tea can be administered to infants using a dropper or spoon. For older children, it can be served warm or cooled in a cup.

When to Use: Fennel can be used when infants or children are experiencing colic, gas, or digestive discomfort. It's also helpful for promoting healthy digestion after meals.

Lemon Balm (Melissa officinalis)

Description: Lemon balm is a mild herb with a gentle lemony flavor. It is known for its calming effects on the nervous system and can help soothe irritability and promote relaxation in infants and children.

Dosage: For infants under 6 months, lemon balm tea can be prepared in small amounts (1-2 teaspoons). For older children, a weaker tea can be given in doses of 1-2 tablespoons.

How to Administer: Lemon balm tea can be administered to infants using a dropper or spoon. For older children, it can be served warm or cooled in a cup.

When to Use: Lemon balm is beneficial for infants and children experiencing restlessness, irritability, or difficulty sleeping. It can also be used to support overall relaxation and well-being.

Ginger (Zingiber officinale)

Description: Ginger is a warming herb with a slightly spicy flavor. It is commonly used to alleviate nausea, aid digestion, and support overall immune health in infants and children.

Dosage: For infants under 6 months, ginger tea can be prepared in small amounts (1-2 teaspoons). For older children, a weaker tea can be given in doses of 1-2 tablespoons.

How to Administer: Ginger tea can be administered to infants using a dropper or spoon. For older children, it can be served warm or cooled in a cup.

When to Use: Ginger can be used when infants or children are experiencing nausea, digestive discomfort, or mild cold symptoms. It's also beneficial for supporting overall immune function and well-being.

Herbs for Adolescents and Adults

Ginseng (Panax ginseng)

Description: Ginseng is an adaptogenic herb known for its ability to enhance energy, reduce fatigue, and improve cognitive function. It has a slightly bitter taste and is available in various forms such as capsules, extracts, and teas.

Dosage: For adolescents and adults, the recommended dosage of ginseng varies depending on the form and concentration. It's generally recommended to start with a lower dosage and gradually increase as needed.

How to Administer: Ginseng can be taken orally in the form of capsules, tablets, or liquid extracts. It can also be brewed as a tea or added to smoothies and other beverages.

When to Use: Ginseng can be used to boost energy, improve focus and concentration, and enhance overall vitality. It's often used by adolescents and adults during periods of stress, fatigue, or mental exhaustion.

Ashwagandha (Withania somnifera)

Description: Ashwagandha is an adaptogenic herb known for its stress-relieving and rejuvenating properties. It has a slightly bitter taste and is available in various forms such as powder, capsules, and liquid extracts.

Dosage: For adolescents and adults, the recommended dosage of ashwagandha varies depending on the form and concentration. It's typically taken in doses ranging from 300 mg to 600 mg per day.

How to Administer: Ashwagandha can be taken orally by mixing the powder into water, juice, or smoothies. You can consume it using capsules or liquid extracts.

When to Use: Ashwagandha can be used to reduce stress, improve mood, and enhance overall well-being. It's often used by adolescents and adults to manage symptoms of anxiety, depression, and fatigue.

Rhodiola (Rhodiola rosea)

Description: Rhodiola is an adaptogenic herb known for its ability to increase energy, reduce fatigue, and improve mental clarity. It has a slightly bitter taste.

Dosage: For adolescents and adults, the recommended dosage of rhodiola varies depending on the form and concentration. It's typically taken in doses ranging from 200 mg to 600 mg per day.

How to Administer: Rhodiola can be taken orally in the form of capsules, tablets, or liquid extracts. It can also be brewed as a tea or added to smoothies and other beverages.

When to Use: Rhodiola can be used to combat fatigue, improve stamina, and enhance cognitive function. It's often used by adolescents and adults to support performance during periods of physical or mental exertion.

Boswellia (Boswellia serrata)

Description: Boswellia is a resin obtained from the Boswellia tree and is commonly used to reduce inflammation and alleviate pain. It has a slightly bitter taste and is available in capsules, extracts, and topical creams.

Dosage: For adolescents and adults, the recommended dosage of boswellia varies depending on the form and concentration. It's typically taken in doses ranging from 300 mg to 1,200 mg per day.

How to Administer: Boswellia can be taken orally in the form of capsules or tablets. It can also be applied topically in the form of creams or ointments for localized pain relief.

When to Use: Boswellia can be used to manage symptoms of inflammatory conditions such as arthritis, osteoarthritis, and inflammatory bowel disease. It's often used by adolescents and adults to reduce pain and improve mobility.

Cat's Claw (Uncaria tomentosa)

Description: Cat's claw originates from the Amazon rainforest and is recognized for its immune-boosting and anti-inflammatory properties. With a mildly bitter flavor, it is available in capsules, extracts, and teas.

Dosage: For adolescents and adults, the recommended dosage is 250 mg to 1,000 mg per day.

How to Administer: Cat's Claw can be taken orally in the form of capsules, tablets, or liquid extracts. It can also be brewed as a tea or added to smoothies and other beverages.

When to Use: Cat's Claw can be used to support immune function, reduce inflammation, and promote overall health. It's often used by adolescents and adults to prevent colds and flu, as well as to manage symptoms of chronic inflammatory conditions.

Considerations for Elderly and Pregnant Women

Ginger (Zingiber officinale)

Description: Ginger is a versatile herb known for its anti-nausea, digestive, and anti-inflammatory properties. It has a spicy, slightly sweet flavor and is available fresh, dried, or as a supplement.

Dosage: For elderly and pregnant women, ginger is generally considered safe when consumed in moderate amounts. A typical dose for nausea relief is 250 mg to 1 gram of powdered ginger or 1 to 2 grams of fresh ginger root.

How to Administer: Ginger can be consumed in various forms, including fresh ginger tea, ginger capsules, or adding grated ginger to meals. Pregnant women should consult their healthcare provider before using ginger supplements or essential oils.

When to Use: Elderly individuals can use ginger to alleviate digestive discomfort, reduce inflammation, and support overall wellness. Pregnant women may use ginger to alleviate nausea and vomiting associated with morning sickness but should do so under the guidance of their healthcare provider.

Peppermint (Mentha piperita)

Description: Peppermint is a refreshing herb known for its ability to relieve digestive issues such as gas, bloating, and indigestion. It has a cooling, minty flavor and is available fresh, dried, or as an essential oil.

Dosage: For elderly and pregnant women, peppermint tea is a safe option for relieving digestive discomfort. It's recommended to drink 1 to 2 cups of peppermint tea per day. Pregnant women should avoid consuming excessive amounts of peppermint essential oil.

How to Administer: Peppermint tea can be made by steeping 1 teaspoon of dried peppermint leaves in hot water for 5 to 10 minutes. Pregnant women should consult their healthcare provider before using peppermint essential oil.

When to Use: Use peppermint tea to reduce digestive problems including gas, bloating, and indigestion. Pregnant women may use peppermint tea to relieve nausea and support healthy digestion but should avoid excessive consumption.

Chamomile (Matricaria chamomilla)

Description: Chamomile is used for its calming and soothing properties. It has a mild, floral flavor and is commonly consumed as a tea.

Dosage: For elderly and pregnant women, chamomile tea is considered safe for regular consumption. It's recommended to drink 1 to 2 cups of chamomile tea per day.

How to Administer: Chamomile tea can be made by steeping 1 to 2 teaspoons of dried chamomile flowers in hot water for 5 to 10 minutes. Pregnant women should avoid chamomile supplements or essential oils.

When to Use: Elderly individuals can use chamomile tea to promote relaxation, reduce stress, and support healthy sleep. Pregnant women may use chamomile tea to alleviate anxiety and promote relaxation but should avoid excessive consumption.

Red Raspberry Leaf (Rubus idaeus)

Description: Red raspberry leaf is a nourishing herb known for its high nutrient content and uterine-toning properties. It has a mildly sweet, earthy flavor and is commonly consumed as a tea.

Dosage: For pregnant women, red raspberry leaf tea is often recommended during the second and third trimesters to support uterine health. It's generally safe to drink 1 to 3 cups of red raspberry leaf tea per day.

How to Administer: Red raspberry leaf tea can be made by steeping 1 to 2 teaspoons of dried red raspberry leaves in hot water for 10 to 15 minutes. Pregnant women should consult their healthcare provider before using red raspberry leaf supplements.

When to Use: Pregnant women can use red raspberry leaf tea to tone the uterus, promote more efficient contractions during labor, and potentially shorten labor duration. It's best to start drinking red raspberry leaf tea gradually in the second trimester and increase the amount as pregnancy progresses.

Nettle (Urtica dioica)

Description: Nettle is a nutritive herb rich in vitamins, minerals, and antioxidants. It has a slightly earthy, grassy flavor and is commonly consumed as tea or used in cooking.

Dosage: For elderly and pregnant women, nettle tea is a safe and nourishing option. It's recommended to drink 1 to 3 cups of nettle tea per day. Pregnant women should avoid consuming excessive amounts of nettle supplements.

How to Administer: Nettle tea can be made by steeping 1 to 2 teaspoons of dried nettle leaves in hot water for 5 to 10 minutes. Pregnant women should consult their healthcare provider before using nettle supplements.

When to Use: Elderly individuals can use nettle tea to support overall health and vitality. Pregnant women may use nettle tea to promote healthy iron levels, reduce leg cramps, and support kidney function, but should avoid excessive consumption.

Part V
THE PROCEDURES, TECHNIQUES, AND TOOLS

Chapter 13
Procedures to Make Herbal Medicines

This chapter will guide you through the process of making various herbal medicines at home. It will cover essential techniques and procedures for creating herbal ointments, preparing herbal syrups, and distilling essential oils.

You will learn about the basic ingredients and tools needed to craft herbal ointments, along with a step-by-step process for making them. Additionally, the chapter will provide insights into storing and using herbal ointments effectively.

This section will provide you with the ingredients required for making herbal syrups, different methods of extraction and preservation, and recipes for crafting common herbal syrups. You'll discover how to extract the beneficial properties of herbs into sweet and palatable syrups.

You will explore the equipment needed and safety precautions to consider when distilling essential oils at home. The chapter will detail distillation techniques and best practices for obtaining high-quality essential oils from aromatic herbs. Additionally, it will provide guidance on storing and utilizing these precious oils effectively.

Making Herbal Ointments

Herbal ointments are versatile preparations that can be used topically to soothe, heal, and protect the skin. Here's a guide on how to make herbal ointments at home:

Basic Ingredients and Tools Needed

Each component plays a crucial role in the process of making herbal ointments:

Carrier Oil

Carrier oils serve as the base of the herbal ointment, diluting the potent herbal extracts and providing a medium for easy application onto the skin. Oils like olive oil, coconut oil, and almond oil are commonly used due to their nourishing properties and ability to absorb herbal constituents effectively.

Beeswax or Carnauba Wax

Beeswax or carnauba wax is added to the ointment mixture to provide texture and consistency. It acts as a natural thickener, helping the ointment solidify and form a stable emulsion. Additionally, beeswax and carnauba wax offer protective properties, forming a barrier on the skin to lock in moisture and prevent moisture loss.

Desired Herbs (dried or fresh)

Herbs are the primary active ingredients in herbal ointments, imparting their medicinal properties to the final product. Whether dried or fresh, herbs contain various compounds such as essential oils, flavonoids, and antioxidants that offer therapeutic benefits for the skin. Different herbs can be chosen based on their specific healing properties, ranging from soothing and anti-inflammatory to antimicrobial and analgesic.

Double Boiler or Heatproof Bowl

A double boiler or heatproof bowl is essential for gently heating and melting the carrier oil and wax without direct exposure to high heat. This ensures that the herbal constituents are preserved and not degraded by excessive temperature, maintaining the potency of the ointment.

Strainer or Cheesecloth

After infusing the carrier oil with herbs, a strainer or cheesecloth is used to separate the herbal matter from the oil, resulting in a smooth and clear herbal infusion. This step ensures that only the beneficial properties of the herbs are retained in the ointment, while any solid particles or debris are filtered out.

Glass Jars or Tins for Storage

Glass jars or tins are used to store the finished herbal ointment. It is important to use non-reactive and airtight containers to preserve the freshness and efficacy of the ointment. Dark-colored jars can also help protect the ointment from light exposure, which can degrade certain herbal compounds over time. Proper storage containers ensure that the ointment remains stable and potent for extended periods.

Step-by-Step Process for Making Ointments

Infusing the Oil

Start by infusing the carrier oil with your chosen herbs. If using dried herbs, fill a glass jar halfway with the herbs and cover with carrier oil. For fresh herbs, ensure they are clean and dry before covering them with oil.

Straining the Oil

After the infusion period, strain the oil using a fine-mesh strainer or cheesecloth to remove the herbal material. Squeeze out as much oil as possible from the herbs.

Melting the Wax: In a double boiler or heatproof bowl placed over a pot of simmering water, melt the beeswax or carnauba wax. Start with a small amount and gradually add more until you reach the desired consistency. Beeswax will create a thicker ointment, while carnauba wax produces a firmer texture.

Combining Ingredients

Once the wax is fully melted, slowly pour in the infused herbal oil while continuously stirring. Mix until well combined and smooth. You can adjust the ratio of oil to wax to achieve the desired thickness.

Cooling and Pouring

Remove the mixture from heat and let it cool slightly before pouring it into clean, dry glass jars or tins. Leave the lids off until the ointment has completely cooled and solidified.

Storing and Using Herbal Ointments

➢ Store your herbal ointments in a cool, dark place to prolong their shelf life. Properly stored ointments can last for several months to a year.

➢ Use a clean spatula or your fingertips to apply the ointment to the affected area as needed. Massage gently until absorbed.

➢ Label your ointments with the ingredients used and the date of preparation for easy identification.

With these simple steps, you can create your own herbal ointments tailored to your specific needs and preferences. Enjoy the therapeutic benefits of nature's healing herbs with homemade herbal preparations.

Preparing Herbal Syrups

Ingredients for Herbal Syrups

Herbal syrups typically consist of three main components: herbs, liquid base, and sweetener. The choice of herbs depends on the desired therapeutic effects, with commonly used herbs including elderberry, echinacea, ginger, and licorice root. The liquid base can be water, glycerin, or apple cider vinegar, while honey or sugar serves as the sweetener.

Herbs

1. Elderberry

Known for its immune-boosting properties, elderberry syrup is made by simmering dried elderberries in water and then adding honey as a sweetener.

2. Echinacea

To prepare echinacea syrup, combine dried echinacea root or flowers with water and simmer until reduced. Add honey for sweetness and strain before bottling.

3. Ginger

Ginger syrup can be made by simmering fresh ginger slices in water, and then adding sugar or honey to taste. It is commonly used for digestive support and to alleviate nausea.

4. Licorice Root

Steep dried licorice root in hot water to extract its sweet and soothing properties. Add honey or sugar and strain before storing.

5. Chamomile

Chamomile syrup is crafted by infusing dried chamomile flowers in warm water and then adding honey for sweetness. It is favored for its calming effects and as a natural remedy for sleep troubles.

Liquid Base

Water

Simple and versatile, water serves as the base for most herbal syrups. It is used to extract the medicinal compounds from herbs through simmering or steeping.

Glycerin

Glycerin-based syrups are alcohol-free and suitable for individuals with alcohol sensitivities. They're made by mixing glycerin with water and herbs, then sweetening to taste.

Apple Cider Vinegar

Apple cider vinegar adds a tangy flavor to syrups and offers additional health benefits. Combine it with water and herbs, then sweeten it with honey for a delicious and nutritious syrup.

Rose Water

Rose water infusions lend a delicate floral aroma and flavor to syrups. They're made by steeping rose petals in hot water, then straining and sweetening with honey or sugar.

Lemon Juice

Adding lemon juice to herbal syrups not only enhances flavor but also provides a boost of vitamin C. Combine it with water, herbs, and sweetener for a refreshing and immune-boosting syrup.

Sweetener

Honey

Honey is a popular natural sweetener for herbal syrups due to its antimicrobial properties and pleasant taste. It is added to hot water infusions of herbs and then strained.

Maple Syrup

Maple syrup adds a rich, caramel-like sweetness to syrups and pairs well with warming herbs like cinnamon and nutmeg. Mix it with water and herbs, then simmer until thickened.

Agave Syrup

Agave syrup is derived from the agave plant and has a mild, neutral flavor. It is used as a vegan alternative to honey and sugar in herbal syrups.

Stevia

Stevia is a calorie-free sweetener derived from the leaves of the Stevia rebaudiana plant. It is highly concentrated, so only a small amount is needed to sweeten herbal syrups.

Cane Sugar

Cane sugar is a classic sweetener for syrups, offering a familiar taste and texture. It is dissolved in hot water along with herbs and then strained before bottling.

Methods of Extraction and Preservation

There are various methods to extract the medicinal properties of herbs for syrups, including decoction, infusion, and maceration. Decoction involves boiling the herbs in water to extract their active compounds, while infusion involves steeping the herbs in hot water or other liquids. Maceration involves soaking the herbs in a liquid base for an extended period to extract their constituents. After extraction, the herbal liquid is strained to remove solid particles and then mixed with a sweetener. Proper preservation techniques, such as refrigeration or adding alcohol, can help extend the shelf life of herbal syrups.

Decoction

A decoction is a simple and effective method for extracting the medicinal properties of herbs by boiling them in water. To prepare a decoction for herbal syrup, combine the desired herbs with water in a pot and bring it to a boil. Once boiling, reduce the heat and allow the mixture to simmer for about 20-30 minutes, or until the liquid is reduced by half. This process helps release the active compounds present in the herbs into the water. After simmering, strain the liquid to remove the solid particles, then mix it with a sweetener of choice to create the syrup.

Example Herbs: Echinacea, ginger, licorice root, astragalus, and cinnamon bark.

Infusion

Infusion involves steeping herbs in hot water or other liquids to extract their medicinal properties. This method is suitable for delicate herbs or flowers that may lose their potency when exposed to high heat. To make an herbal infusion for syrup, place the desired herbs in a heatproof container and cover them with hot water. Allow the herbs to steep for 15-30 minutes, depending on the desired strength of the infusion. Once steeped, strain the liquid and combine it with a sweetener to create the syrup.

Example Herbs: Chamomile flowers, lavender buds, peppermint leaves, rose petals, and lemon balm.

Maceration

Maceration involves soaking herbs in a liquid base, such as alcohol, glycerin, or vinegar, to extract their medicinal constituents over time. This method is ideal for extracting both water-soluble and oil-soluble compounds from herbs. To prepare an herbal maceration for syrup, place the desired herbs in a clean glass jar and cover them with the chosen liquid base. Seal the jar tightly and store it in a cool, dark place for several weeks, shaking it occasionally to agitate the mixture. Once the maceration period is complete, strain the liquid and mix it with a sweetener to create the syrup.

Example Herbs: Elderberries, echinacea roots, garlic cloves, hawthorn berries, and marshmallow root.

Cold Water Infusion

Cold water infusion is a gentle method for extracting the medicinal properties of herbs without applying heat. This method is suitable for herbs that are sensitive to heat or volatile compounds that may evaporate at high temperatures. To make a cold water infusion for syrup, place the desired herbs in a glass jar and cover them with cold water. Seal the jar and let it sit in the refrigerator for 8-12 hours or overnight. After steeping, strain the liquid and mix it with a sweetener to create the syrup.

Example Herbs: Dandelion roots, burdock roots, nettle leaves, oat straw, and cleavers.

Combination Methods

Some herbal syrups may benefit from a combination of extraction methods to extract a wide range of active compounds. For example, you may start with a decoction to extract the water-soluble constituents of the herbs, then combine it with a maceration of oil-soluble herbs to create a more comprehensive syrup. Experiment with different combinations and extraction techniques to find the most effective method for your desired herbal syrup.

Example Herbs: Ginger (decoction) combined with lemon peel (maceration), elderberries (cold water infusion) with echinacea roots (decoction), cinnamon bark (infusion) with cloves (maceration), chamomile flowers (infusion) with lavender buds (maceration), and marshmallow root (decoction) with licorice root (maceration).

Methods of Preservation

Refrigeration

Refrigeration is one of the simplest and most effective methods to preserve herbal syrups. After preparing the syrup, store it in a clean glass jar or bottle and place it in the refrigerator. The cold temperature helps slow down microbial growth and oxidation, extending the shelf life of the syrup. Make sure to use airtight containers to prevent moisture and contaminants from entering the syrup.

Adding Alcohol

Adding alcohol to herbal syrups can help inhibit the growth of bacteria and fungi, thereby extending their shelf life. Alcohol acts as a natural preservative and also helps extract and preserve certain active compounds from the herbs. Common types of alcohol used for preservation include vodka, brandy, or rum. To preserve the syrup, add alcohol to the mixture before bottling it. The alcohol content should be at least 20-25% to ensure effective preservation.

Pasteurization

Pasteurization is a heat treatment process that helps kill harmful microorganisms in food and beverages, thereby prolonging their shelf life. To pasteurize herbal syrups, heat the syrup to a temperature of 160°F (71°C) and maintain it at this temperature for at least 5 minutes. Use a thermometer to monitor the temperature accurately and avoid overheating, as it may degrade the quality of the syrup. After pasteurization, immediately transfer the syrup to sterilized bottles or jars and seal them tightly to prevent contamination.

Freezing

Freezing is another method to preserve herbal syrups for long-term storage. After preparing the syrup, allow it to cool to room temperature, then pour it into ice cube trays or freezer-safe containers. Cover the containers tightly to prevent freezer burn and store them in the freezer. Freezing helps slow down enzymatic reactions and microbial growth, keeping the syrup fresh for several months. When needed, thaw the syrup in the refrigerator overnight or at room temperature for a few hours before use.

pH Adjustment

pH adjustment involves altering the acidity or alkalinity of the syrup to create an environment that inhibits microbial growth. Most microorganisms thrive in neutral or slightly acidic environments, so lowering the pH of the syrup can help prevent spoilage. Adding acidic ingredients such as lemon juice or citric acid can lower the pH of the syrup and enhance its shelf life. Measure the pH of the syrup using a pH meter or pH test strips and adjust it as needed to achieve a pH below 4.0, which is considered safe for preservation.

Recipes for Common Herbal Syrups

There are numerous recipes for herbal syrups targeting specific health concerns. For example, elderberry syrup is often used to boost the immune system and alleviate cold and flu symptoms. To make elderberry syrup, dried elderberries are simmered with water and then strained. The liquid is mixed with honey and simmered until thickened to create a syrup. Similarly, ginger syrup can be made by simmering fresh ginger root in water and then mixing the infused liquid with honey or sugar. Other common herbal syrup recipes include echinacea syrup for immune support and licorice root syrup for soothing sore throats.

Elderberry Syrup

Ingredients:

1 cup dried elderberries

3 cups water

1 cup honey

Optional: cinnamon sticks, ginger slices

Method:

➢ In a pot, combine elderberries, water, and optional spices (cinnamon sticks, ginger slices).

➢ Start boiling and then reduce heat and simmer for at least 40 minutes. Make sure desiring this time the liquid is reduced by half.

➢ Remove and strain the liquid using a fine mesh strainer or cheesecloth.

➢ Allow the liquid to cool slightly, then stir in honey until fully dissolved.

➢ Transfer the syrup to a clean glass jar or bottle and store it in the refrigerator.

Usage:

Adults: Take 1 tablespoon daily for immune support during cold and flu season.

Children (over 1 year old): Take 1 teaspoon daily. Adjust dosage based on weight and age.

Infants (under 1-year-old): Consult a pediatrician before giving elderberry syrup to infants.

Ginger Lemon Syrup

Ingredients:

1 cup fresh ginger root, sliced

1 cup honey

1 cup water

Juice of 1 lemon

Lemon zest (optional)

Method:

➢ In a pot, combine ginger slices, water, lemon juice, and lemon zest.

➢ Boil and simmer for half hour.

➢ Allow the liquid to cool slightly, then stir in honey until fully dissolved.

➢ Transfer the syrup to a clean glass jar or bottle and store it in the refrigerator.

Usage:

Adults: Take 1 tablespoon daily for immune support and digestive health.

Children (over 1 year old): Take 1 teaspoon daily. Adjust dosage based on weight and age.

Infants (under 1 year old): Avoid giving ginger syrup to infants due to potential choking hazards.

Chamomile Lavender Syrup

Ingredients:

1/4 cup dried chamomile flowers

1/4 cup dried lavender buds

2 cups water

1 cup honey

Method:

- ➢ In a pot, combine chamomile flowers, lavender buds, and water.
- ➢ Bring the mixture to a gentle simmer and let it infuse for 20-30 minutes.
- ➢ Remove from heat and strain the liquid using a fine mesh strainer or cheesecloth.
- ➢ Allow the liquid to cool slightly, then stir in honey until fully dissolved.
- ➢ Transfer the syrup to a clean glass jar or bottle and store it in the refrigerator.

Usage:

Adults: Take 1 tablespoon before bedtime for relaxation and sleep support.

Children (over 1 year old): Take 1 teaspoon before bedtime. Adjust dosage based on weight and age.

Infants (under 1 year old): Avoid giving chamomile lavender syrup to infants due to potential allergic reactions.

Lemon Thyme Honey Syrup

Ingredients:

1/4 cup fresh thyme leaves

1 cup honey

Zest of 1 lemon

1 cup water

Method:

- ➢ In a pot, combine thyme leaves, lemon zest, and water.
- ➢ Bring the mixture to a boil, then reduce heat and simmer for 15-20 minutes.
- ➢ Remove from heat and strain the liquid using a fine mesh strainer or cheesecloth.
- ➢ Allow the liquid to cool slightly, then stir in honey until fully dissolved.
- ➢ Transfer the syrup to a clean glass jar or bottle and store it in the refrigerator.

Usage:

Adults: Take 1 tablespoon daily for immune support and respiratory health.

Children (over 1 year old): Take 1 teaspoon daily. Adjust dosage based on weight and age.

Infants (under 1 year old): Avoid giving lemon thyme syrup to infants due to potential allergic reactions.

Rosehip Hibiscus Syrup

Ingredients:

1/2 cup dried rosehips

1/4 cup dried hibiscus flowers

2 cups water

1 cup honey

Method:

➢ In a saucepan, combine rosehips, hibiscus flowers, and water.
➢ Bring the mixture to a gentle simmer and let it infuse for 20-30 minutes.
➢ Remove from heat and strain the liquid using a fine mesh strainer or cheesecloth.
➢ Allow the liquid to cool slightly, then stir in honey until fully dissolved.
➢ Transfer the syrup to a clean glass jar or bottle and store it in the refrigerator.

Usage:

Adults: Take 1 tablespoon daily for immune support and antioxidant benefits.

Children (over 1 year old): Take 1 teaspoon daily. Adjust dosage based on weight and age.

Turmeric Honey Syrup

Ingredients:

1/4 cup fresh turmeric root, thinly sliced

1 cup honey

1 cup water

Black pepper (optional)

Method:

➢ In a saucepan, combine turmeric slices, water, and optional black pepper.
➢ Bring the mixture to a gentle simmer and let it cook for 20-30 minutes.
➢ Remove from heat and strain the liquid using a fine mesh strainer or cheesecloth.
➢ Allow the liquid to cool slightly, then stir in honey until fully dissolved.
➢ Transfer the syrup to a clean glass jar or bottle and store it in the refrigerator.

Usage:

Adults: Take 1 tablespoon daily for its anti-inflammatory and immune-boosting properties.

Children (over 1 year old): Take 1 teaspoon daily. Adjust dosage based on weight and age.

Infants (under 1 year old): Avoid giving turmeric syrup to infants due to potential allergic reactions.

Nettle Mint Syrup

Ingredients:

1/2 cup dried nettle leaves

1/4 cup fresh mint leaves

2 cups water

1 cup honey

Method:

- ➢ In a saucepan, combine nettle leaves, mint leaves, and water.
- ➢ Bring the mixture to a gentle simmer and let it infuse for 20-30 minutes.
- ➢ Remove from heat and strain the liquid using a fine mesh strainer or cheesecloth.
- ➢ Allow the liquid to cool slightly, then stir in honey until fully dissolved.
- ➢ Transfer the syrup to a clean glass jar or bottle and store it in the refrigerator.

Usage:

Adults: Take 1 tablespoon daily for its antioxidant and anti-allergic properties.

Children (over 1 year old): Take 1 teaspoon daily. Adjust dosage based on weight and age.

Infants (under 1 year old): Avoid giving nettle mint syrup to infants due to potential allergic reactions.

Lemon Echinacea Syrup

Ingredients:

1/4 cup dried echinacea root

Zest of 2 lemons

Juice of 2 lemons

1 cup honey

2 cups water

Method:

- ➢ In a saucepan, combine echinacea root, lemon zest, lemon juice, and water.
- ➢ Bring the mixture to a gentle simmer and let it infuse for 20-30 minutes.
- ➢ Remove from heat and strain the liquid using a fine mesh strainer or cheesecloth.

- ➤ Allow the liquid to cool slightly, then stir in honey until fully dissolved.
- ➤ Transfer the syrup to a clean glass jar or bottle and store it in the refrigerator.

Usage:

Adults: Take 1 tablespoon daily for immune support during cold and flu season.

Children (over 1 year old): Take 1 teaspoon daily. Adjust dosage based on weight and age.

Infants (under 1 year old): Avoid giving lemon echinacea syrup to infants due to potential allergic reactions.

Rosemary Thyme Syrup

Ingredients:

1/4 cup fresh rosemary leaves

1/4 cup fresh thyme leaves

1 cup honey

2 cups water

Method:

- ➤ In a saucepan, combine rosemary leaves, thyme leaves, and water.
- ➤ Bring the mixture to a gentle simmer and let it infuse for 20-30 minutes.
- ➤ Remove from heat and strain the liquid using a fine mesh strainer or cheesecloth.
- ➤ Allow the liquid to cool slightly, then stir in honey until fully dissolved.
- ➤ Transfer the syrup to a clean glass jar or bottle and store it in the refrigerator.

Usage:

Adults: Take 1 tablespoon daily for its antioxidant and antimicrobial properties.

Children (over 1 year old): Take 1 teaspoon daily. Adjust dosage based on weight and age.

Infants (under 1 year old): Avoid giving rosemary thyme syrup to infants due to potential allergic reactions.

Cranberry Orange Syrup

Ingredients:

1/2 cup dried cranberries

Zest of 1 orange

Juice of 1 orange

1 cup honey

2 cups water

Method:

- In a pot, combine dried cranberries, orange zest, orange juice, and water.
- Bring the mixture to a gentle simmer and let it cook for 20-30 minutes.
- Remove from heat and strain the liquid using a fine mesh strainer or cheesecloth.
- Allow the liquid to cool slightly, then stir in honey until fully dissolved.
- Transfer the syrup to a clean glass jar or bottle and store it in the refrigerator.

Usage:

Adults: Take 1 tablespoon daily.

Distilling Essential Oils

Distilling essential oils is a process of extracting aromatic compounds from plants to create concentrated oils with therapeutic properties. Here's what you need to know:

Equipment and Safety Precautions

Distillation Apparatus: The distillation apparatus is the primary equipment used for distilling essential oils. It typically consists of three main components:

Still or Distillation Unit: This is the main vessel where the botanical material is heated to produce steam.

Condenser: The condenser cools the steam, causing it to condense back into liquid form. It consists of a tube or coil through which cold water flows.

Collection Vessel: This is where the condensed essential oil collects after passing through the condenser.

Heat Source: A reliable heat source is essential for heating the water in the distillation apparatus and generating steam. Common heat sources include:

Stove: A gas or electric stove can provide consistent heat for the distillation process.

Hot Plate: A hot plate is a portable electric appliance that can be used as an alternative heat source.

Glass Bottles or Vials: Glass bottles or vials are used to store the distilled essential oils after the distillation process. It is essential to use dark-colored glass bottles to protect the oils from degradation due to light exposure. Amber or cobalt blue glass bottles are commonly used for this purpose.

Safety Gear: When distilling essential oils, it's crucial to prioritize safety to prevent accidents and injuries. Here are some safety precautions to follow:

Gloves: Wear heat-resistant gloves to protect your hands from burns and scalds during the distillation process.

Safety Goggles: Safety goggles or glasses with side shields should be worn to protect your eyes from exposure to hot steam and potential splashes of essential oils.

Apron: Wearing an apron can help protect your clothing from spills and stains.

Ventilation: Ensure adequate ventilation in the distillation area to prevent the buildup of steam and essential oil vapors, which can cause respiratory irritation.

Distillation Techniques and Best Practices

Selection of Botanical Material

Choose high-quality botanical material for distillation to ensure the production of potent and aromatic essential oils. Fresh or dried herbs, flowers, roots, and other plant parts can be used for distillation. Select plants that are free from mold, pests, and diseases, as these can affect the quality of the final essential oil.

Choose high-quality botanical material for distillation to ensure the production of potent and aromatic essential oils.

Examples:

Lavender: Select fresh lavender flowers with vibrant color and strong fragrances for optimal oil yield.

Peppermint: Harvest peppermint leaves just before flowering to capture the highest concentration of essential oils.

Eucalyptus: Collect eucalyptus leaves from mature trees, preferably in the early morning when oil content is highest.

Preparation of Botanical Material

Proper preparation of the botanical material is essential for optimal extraction of essential oils. Depending on the plant species, the material may need to be chopped, crushed, or ground to increase the surface area and facilitate the release of aromatic compounds during distillation. Ensure uniformity in the size and texture of the botanical material to achieve consistent results.

➢ Clean the botanical material to remove dirt, debris, and pests that may contaminate the essential oil.

➢ Dry the herbs thoroughly to reduce moisture content, as excess moisture can affect the quality of the distilled oil.

Examples:

Lavender: Remove any damaged or discolored flowers and spread them out in a single layer. Make sure to dry in a cool and open or ventilated area.

Peppermint: Wash peppermint leaves gently under running water and pat them dry with a clean cloth or paper towel before use.

Eucalyptus: Trim eucalyptus branches to remove any dead or diseased leaves, and allow them to air dry completely before distillation.

Loading the Still

Carefully load the prepared botanical material into the still or distillation unit. Avoid overfilling the still, as this can impede the flow of steam and compromise the efficiency of the distillation process. Maintain a balanced ratio of botanical material to water to ensure adequate extraction of essential oils.

➤ Set up the distillation apparatus according to manufacturer instructions, ensuring a tight seal to prevent steam from escaping.

➤ Add the prepared botanical material to the distillation unit and fill the collection vessel with cold water.

➤ Apply heat gradually to the still, allowing the water to heat up and produce steam, which carries the essential oil vapors through the condenser.

Examples:

Lavender: Place fresh lavender flowers in the distillation unit and heat the water slowly to release the aromatic essential oils.

Peppermint: Add peppermint leaves to the still and adjust the heat to maintain a steady flow of steam for efficient extraction of oils.

Eucalyptus: Load eucalyptus leaves into the distillation apparatus and monitor the temperature closely to prevent overheating and degradation of oils.

Water Quality

Use high-quality, preferably distilled or purified water for the distillation process. Water quality can significantly impact the aroma and purity of the resulting essential oil. Avoid using chlorinated or heavily mineralized water, as these impurities can affect the fragrance and therapeutic properties of the oil.

Lavender

Distilled Water - Lavender essential oil is prized for its delicate floral scent and therapeutic benefits. Using distilled water ensures that no impurities or contaminants interfere with the extraction process, resulting in a purer and more aromatic oil.

Spring Water-Natural Spring water is another excellent choice for distilling lavender essential oil. It is free from additives and chemicals, preserving the integrity of the floral fragrance and therapeutic properties of the oil.

Filtered Water - If distilled or spring water is not available, filtered water can be used as an alternative. Filtering removes common contaminants, such as chlorine and sediment, improving the overall quality of the distilled lavender essential oil.

Peppermint

Purified Water - Peppermint essential oil is valued for its invigorating scent and cooling properties. Purified water ensures that no unwanted odors or flavors are introduced during the distillation process, resulting in clean and refreshing oil.

Reverse Osmosis Water - Reverse osmosis water undergoes a filtration process that removes impurities and minerals, making it an ideal choice for distilling peppermint essential oil. It helps maintain the purity and potency of the oil's aroma and therapeutic benefits.

Spring Water - Like lavender, peppermint essential oil can also be distilled using natural spring water. The pristine quality of spring water enhances the freshness and vitality of the oil, capturing the essence of the peppermint plant.

Eucalyptus

Distilled Water - Eucalyptus essential oil is renowned for its crisp, camphoraceous aroma and respiratory benefits. Distilled water ensures that the oil remains free from impurities, preserving its clarifying scent and therapeutic properties.

Filtered Water - Filtered water is a suitable option for distilling eucalyptus essential oil, especially if distilled or spring water is unavailable. Filtering removes contaminants, ensuring a clean and aromatic oil suitable for aromatherapy and respiratory support.

Rainwater - In areas with clean air and minimal pollution, rainwater can be collected and used for distilling eucalyptus essential oil. Rainwater is naturally pure and free from additives, making it an eco-friendly option for botanical extraction.

Heating the Still

Gradually heat the still to generate steam and initiate the distillation process. Start with a low to medium heat setting to prevent rapid boiling, which can cause excessive agitation and potential loss of volatile compounds. Monitor the temperature closely and adjust as needed to maintain a gentle simmer.

Condensation and Collection

As steam rises from the boiling botanical material, it passes through the condenser, where it is cooled and condensed back into liquid form. Ensure that the condenser is properly connected and functioning effectively to capture the condensed essential oil. Use a collection vessel to collect the aromatic distillate.

Examples of Collection

Lavender

Traditional Alembic Still - In traditional distillation setups like an alembic still, steam rises from the lavender botanicals and enters the condenser. The condenser cools the steam, causing it to condense into liquid form. The condensed lavender essential oil then drips into a collection vessel placed below the condenser, ready for further processing or storage.

Modern Distillation Apparatus - In modern distillation setups, such as a steam distillation apparatus, the process is similar. The steam containing lavender essential oil vapor travels through the condenser, where it undergoes condensation. The resulting liquid, a mixture of water and essential oil, is collected in a separator, allowing the oil to separate and float on top for easy extraction.

Homemade Distillation Setup - For DIY enthusiasts, a simple distillation setup can be created using household items. A pot filled with lavender and water is heated, producing steam that travels through a tube to a condenser. The condenser, often a coil immersed in cold water, causes the steam to condense, with the resulting lavender essential oil collected in a glass vessel placed at the end of the condenser.

Peppermint

Copper Alembic Still - Copper alembic stills are commonly used for distilling peppermint essential oil. As steam rises from the peppermint leaves and stems, it enters the condenser, where it cools and condenses. The condensed essential oil then drips into a collection vessel, separated from the hydrosol, which is collected separately.

Fractional Distillation Setup - In larger-scale distillation operations, a fractional distillation setup may be used for peppermint essential oil extraction. This setup allows for precise control over temperature and pressure, resulting in high-quality oil with consistent aroma and potency. The condensed oil is collected in a receiver flask, ready for further processing or bottling.

Steam Distillation Apparatus - A steam distillation apparatus is another effective method for extracting peppermint essential oil. Steam generated from boiling water passes through the peppermint plant material, carrying the essential oil vapor. As it enters the condenser, the steam condenses, and the resulting oil-water mixture is collected in a separator. The peppermint oil separates and floats on top, allowing for easy collection.

Eucalyptus

Modular Distillation System - In industrial settings, a modular distillation system may be used for eucalyptus essential oil production. Steam generated from boiling eucalyptus leaves and branches passes through the condenser, where it condenses into a liquid. The condensed eucalyptus oil is collected in a separate vessel, while the hydrosol is collected for other purposes.

Vacuum Distillation Setup - Vacuum distillation is a technique commonly employed for extracting sensitive essential oils like eucalyptus oil. By operating under reduced pressure, the boiling point of the oil is lowered, minimizing thermal degradation. The condensed oil is collected in a receiver flask, ensuring maximum preservation of its aroma and therapeutic properties.

Solar Still - In regions with abundant sunlight, solar still can be used to distill eucalyptus essential oil. The sun's heat evaporates water from the eucalyptus material, creating steam that travels to the condenser. As the steam cools and condenses, the resulting eucalyptus oil is collected in a reservoir, ready for use in aromatherapy or medicinal applications.

Distillation Duration

The duration of distillation varies depending on the botanical material and the desired potency of the essential oil. Some plants release their aromatic compounds quickly, while others require longer distillation times for optimal extraction. Monitor the distillation process closely and adjust the duration accordingly.

Distillation duration refers to the length of time that botanical material is subjected to the distillation process to extract essential oils effectively. The duration can vary depending on factors such as the type of botanical material, its moisture content, and the desired potency of the resulting essential oil. Here's an explanation with examples of three herbs:

Lavender

Lavender typically requires a distillation duration of about 1.5 to 2 hours to extract its essential oil fully.

During this time, steam is passed through the lavender flowers and stems, allowing the aromatic compounds to vaporize and travel through the condenser.

The duration ensures that the steam effectively penetrates the lavender material, extracting the maximum amount of essential oil without overheating or damaging its delicate constituents.

Longer distillation periods may lead to degradation of the oil's fragrance and therapeutic properties, while shorter durations may result in incomplete extraction.

Peppermint

Peppermint distillation typically lasts between 1 to 1.5 hours to extract its essential oil fully.

The duration allows sufficient time for the steam to permeate through the peppermint leaves and stems, carrying the volatile oils along with it.

It's essential to monitor the distillation closely to prevent overheating, as excessive heat can cause the oil to degrade and lose its characteristic aroma and efficacy.

Shorter distillation times may result in lower oil yields, while prolonged durations can lead to the breakdown of sensitive compounds, affecting the overall quality of the oil.

Eucalyptus

Eucalyptus distillation typically ranges from 2 to 3 hours to ensure the complete extraction of its essential oil.

The longer duration is necessary due to the denser nature of eucalyptus leaves and branches, which require more time for the steam to penetrate and extract the oils.

During the distillation process, it's crucial to maintain stable temperature and pressure conditions to optimize oil yield and quality.

While shorter distillation times may yield some oil, they may not capture the full spectrum of eucalyptus's therapeutic compounds. Conversely, excessively long durations can lead to the degradation of delicate constituents, compromising the oil's effectiveness.

Temperature Control

Maintain consistent temperature control throughout the distillation process to prevent overheating or boiling over. Avoid sudden temperature fluctuations, as these can impact the quality and aroma of the essential oil. Use a thermometer to monitor the temperature of the still and make necessary adjustments.

Monitoring Progress

Regularly monitor the progress of the distillation process by observing the volume and clarity of the collected distillate. Keep track of the aroma intensity and color of the oil, as these indicators can help determine when the distillation is complete. Exercise patience and allow sufficient time for the extraction of essential oils.

Post-Distillation Care

Once distillation is complete, carefully remove the collection vessel and allow the essential oil to cool to room temperature. Transfer the oil to dark-colored glass bottles or vials for storage, ensuring a tight seal to prevent oxidation and evaporation. Label each bottle with the botanical name, date of distillation, and any other relevant information. Store the essential oils in a cool, dark place away from direct sunlight and heat sources to preserve their freshness and potency.

Storing and Using Essential Oils

Storage: Essential oils should be stored in dark-colored glass bottles or vials to protect them from light and heat. Keep them tightly sealed and away from direct sunlight.

Dilution: Essential oils are highly concentrated and should be diluted before use. Use a carrier oil such as jojoba oil or coconut oil to dilute essential oils for topical application.

Inhalation: Add a few drops of essential oil to a diffuser or inhale the aroma directly from the bottle to experience its therapeutic effects.

Topical Application: Dilute essential oils in a carrier oil and apply them to the skin for massage or to target specific areas of concern.

Safety Precautions: Some essential oils may cause skin irritation or sensitization. Always perform a patch test before using a new essential oil and discontinue use if irritation occurs. Keep essential oils out of reach of children and pets.

Chapter 14
Tools and Techniques for Home Gardening

In this chapter, you will explore the essential tools and techniques needed for successful home gardening, catering to both beginners and experienced gardeners alike.

Tools Required for Home Gardening

Gardening is a rewarding and fulfilling hobby that can be enjoyed by individuals of all skill levels. To get started, beginners will need a basic set of gardening tools, while experienced gardeners may require more specialized equipment to maintain and enhance their garden. Here is an overview of the tools required for home gardening:

Essential Gardening Tools for Beginners

Hand Trowel

A hand trowel is a small, handheld tool with a pointed blade used for digging small holes, transplanting seedlings, and removing weeds.

Garden Fork

A garden fork is essential for breaking up soil, aerating the ground, and turning compost. It typically has sturdy tines and a D-shaped handle for comfortable grip.

Pruning Shears

Pruning shears, also known as secateurs, are used for trimming and shaping plants, removing dead or damaged branches, and harvesting fruits and flowers.

Garden Gloves

Garden gloves protect your hands from thorns, sharp edges, and abrasive surfaces while working in the garden. Choose gloves made from durable, breathable materials for comfort and protection.

Watering Can or Hose

A watering can or hose is essential for watering plants, ensuring they receive an adequate supply of moisture for healthy growth.

Garden Rake

A garden rake is used for leveling soil, removing debris, and spreading mulch or compost. Choose a rake with sturdy tines and a comfortable handle grip.

Garden Hoe

A garden hoe is useful for cultivating soil, removing weeds, and creating furrows for planting seeds or seedlings.

Garden Spade

A garden spade is a larger digging tool used for digging planting holes, edging borders, and lifting soil or compost.

Pruning Saw

A pruning saw is a useful tool for cutting through thick branches and woody stems that are too large for pruning shears.

Garden Kneeler or Pad

A garden kneeler or pad provides cushioning and support for your knees while working close to the ground, reducing strain and discomfort.

Advanced Tools for Experienced Gardeners

Soil Testing Kit

A soil testing kit allows experienced gardeners to analyze the pH level and nutrient content of their soil, enabling them to make informed decisions about fertilization and soil amendment.

Garden Forklift

A garden forklift is a specialized tool that makes it easier to lift and transport heavy pots, bags of soil, or other gardening supplies.

Electric Pruning Shears

Electric pruning shears are powered by electricity or batteries and make pruning large or dense shrubs and trees more efficient and less labor-intensive.

Drip Irrigation System

A drip irrigation system delivers water directly to the roots of plants through a network of hoses and emitters, conserving water and ensuring efficient watering.

Garden Cart or Wheelbarrow

A garden cart or wheelbarrow is essential for transporting tools, plants, and other heavy items around the garden, reducing strain on the body and making gardening tasks more manageable.

Procedures and Requirements to Grow Herbs

Growing herbs can be a fulfilling and rewarding experience, whether you have a sprawling garden or just a few pots on your windowsill. To ensure successful herb cultivation, it's essential to understand the procedures and requirements involved. This chapter will delve into soil preparation and fertilization, planting techniques for different herbs, and watering and maintenance schedules.

Soil Preparation and Fertilization

Soil Type: Herbs thrive in well-draining soil that is rich in organic matter. Before planting, assess your soil type and amend it if necessary. Sandy soils benefit from the addition of compost or aged manure to improve water retention, while heavy clay soils require organic matter to enhance drainage.

pH Level: Most herbs prefer a slightly acidic to neutral pH range of 6.0 to 7.0. Test your soil's pH level using a soil testing kit and adjust it as needed with amendments such as lime (to raise pH) or elemental sulfur (to lower pH).

Fertilization: Herbs are generally light feeders and do not require heavy fertilization. Incorporate a balanced, slow-release fertilizer or organic compost into the soil before planting to provide essential nutrients. Avoid over-fertilizing, as this can lead to excessive leaf growth at the expense of flavor and aroma.

Planting Techniques for Different Herbs

Seed Starting vs. Transplants

Some herbs, such as basil and dill, are best started from seeds directly sown into the garden, while others, like rosemary and thyme, are often purchased as transplants from nurseries. Follow seed packet instructions for proper planting depth and spacing.

Spacing

Proper spacing is crucial to ensure adequate airflow and prevent overcrowding, which can lead to disease and pest issues. Space herbs according to their mature size, typically ranging from 6 inches to 2 feet apart, depending on the variety.

Container Gardening

Herbs can also be grown in containers, making them suitable for small spaces or indoor cultivation. Choose containers with adequate drainage holes and fill them with a high-quality potting mix. Place pots in a sunny location and water regularly to keep the soil evenly moist.

Watering and Maintenance Schedules

Watering

Herbs prefer consistently moist but not waterlogged soil. Water newly planted herbs deeply to establish roots, then gradually reduce frequency as they become established. Water early in the day to minimize evaporation and reduce the risk of fungal diseases.

Harvesting

Regular pruning encourages bushy growth and prolongs the harvest season. Pinch back the tips of herbs like basil and mint to promote branching, and harvest leaves as needed for culinary use. Remove any dead or yellowing foliage to maintain plant health.

Harvesting and Preserving Herbs

Harvesting and preserving herbs are essential skills for any herb gardener. Knowing the optimal harvest times and techniques ensures that you can enjoy your homegrown herbs at their peak flavor and potency. In this chapter, we'll explore the best practices for harvesting different parts of herbs and various methods for preserving them for long-term storage.

Optimal Harvest Times for Various Herbs

Leafy Herbs

Harvest leafy herbs like basil, parsley, and cilantro when they reach their peak growth and before they start to flower. For most leafy herbs, this is typically in the morning after the dew has dried but before the sun becomes too intense.

Flowering Herbs

Flowers should be harvested just as they begin to open fully, as this is when they contain the highest concentration of essential oils and flavor compounds. Examples include chamomile, lavender, and calendula.

Root Herbs

Root herbs such as ginger, turmeric, and dandelion should be harvested in the fall after the foliage has died back. This allows the plant to store maximum energy in the roots.

Techniques for Harvesting Leaves, Flowers, Roots, and Seeds

Leaves

Use sharp, clean scissors or pruning shears to snip leaves just above a leaf node or set of leaves. This encourages bushy growth and allows the plant to recover quickly.

Flowers

Harvest flowers by gently pinching or cutting the stem just below the flower head. Be careful not to damage surrounding foliage or buds.

Roots

For root herbs, carefully dig around the base of the plant with a garden fork or shovel to loosen the soil, then gently lift the plant from the ground. Shake off excess soil and trim any long roots before washing and drying.

Seeds

Allow seed pods to mature fully on the plant before harvesting. Collect seeds by gently shaking or tapping the pods over a clean container to release them.

Drying and Curing Methods for Long-term Storage

Air Drying

Lay harvested herbs in a single layer on a clean, dry surface away from direct sunlight. Allow them to air dry until crisp, then store them in airtight containers in a cool, dark place.

Oven Drying

Spread herbs on a baking sheet and place them in an oven set to the lowest temperature (around 100-120°F or 40-50°C) with the door slightly ajar. Check frequently and remove when dry.

Dehydrator

Use a food dehydrator set to the appropriate temperature for herbs (typically around 95°F or 35°C) to dry herbs quickly and evenly.

Preservation Methods for Herbs

Preserving herbs allows you to extend their shelf life and enjoy their benefits long after the growing season has ended. In this chapter, we'll explore various preservation methods, including drying, freezing, and creating herbal extracts, tinctures, and infusions.

Drying, Freezing, and Storing Herbs

Drying Herbs

Air drying is one of the oldest and simplest methods of preserving herbs. To dry herbs, tie small bunches together and hang them upside down in a warm, dry location with good air circulation. Alternatively, you can spread herbs on a drying rack or tray. Once dry, store them in airtight containers away from light and moisture.

Freezing Herbs

Freezing is another effective way to preserve herbs while retaining their flavor and aroma. Wash and pat dry fresh herbs, then chop or leave them whole before freezing. Place herbs in an airtight container or freezer bag and store them in the freezer. Frozen herbs can be added directly to dishes without thawing.

Making Tinctures and Infusions

Tinctures

Tinctures are concentrated herbal extracts made by soaking herbs in alcohol or glycerin. To make a tincture, finely chop or grind dried herbs. Place them in a glass jar. Cover the herbs with alcohol. Ensure that they are fully submerged. Seal the jar and let it sit for several weeks, shaking it occasionally. After the steeping period, strain the liquid through a fine mesh sieve or cheesecloth and store the tincture in dark glass bottles.

Infusions

Herbal infusions are made by steeping herbs in hot water to extract their flavors and medicinal properties. To make an infusion, place dried or fresh herbs in a heatproof container and cover them with boiling water. Let the herbs steep for 10-15 minutes, then strain the liquid and discard the herbs. Infusions can be enjoyed as a hot tea or used as a base for other herbal preparations.

Creating Herbal Extracts and Powders

Herbal Extracts

Herbal extracts are concentrated liquid preparations made by extracting the active compounds from herbs using alcohol, glycerin, or vinegar. To make an extract, finely chop or grind dried herbs and place them in a glass jar. Cover the herbs with the solvent of your choice and let them steep for several weeks, shaking the jar regularly. After the steeping period, strain the liquid and store the extract in dark glass bottles.

Herbal Powders

Herbal powders are made by grinding dried herbs into a fine powder using a mortar and pestle or electric grinder. Powders can be used to make capsules, and herbal teas, or added to food and beverages for flavor and health benefits. Store herbal powders in airtight containers away from light and moisture to preserve their potency.

BONUS
Herbal Supplements

Herbal supplements for meals are natural substances derived from plants that are consumed alongside regular food to enhance nutritional intake and promote overall well-being. These supplements can be in various forms, including powders, capsules, extracts, or teas. They are typically rich in vitamins, minerals, antioxidants, and other bioactive compounds that offer numerous health benefits.

10 Benefits of Herbal Supplements

Benefits of incorporating herbal supplements into meals:

1. Nutritional Boost

Herbal supplements are often packed with essential vitamins, minerals, and nutrients that may be lacking in the diet, providing a convenient way to fill nutritional gaps.

2. Antioxidant Support

Many herbs contain potent antioxidants that help combat oxidative stress and neutralize harmful free radicals in the body, reducing the risk of chronic diseases and supporting overall health.

3. Digestive Aid

Certain herbs possess digestive properties that can help alleviate digestive discomfort, promote healthy digestion, and soothe gastrointestinal issues like bloating, gas, and indigestion.

4. Immune System Support

Several herbs are very effective in boosting immunity.

5. Anti-inflammatory Effects

Many herbs exhibit anti-inflammatory properties, which can help reduce inflammation in the body, alleviate pain and stiffness, and support joint and muscle health.

6. Stress Reduction

Certain herbs contain adaptogenic compounds that help the body adapt to stress and promote a sense of calm and relaxation, helping to reduce stress levels and improve overall well-being.

7. Heart Health

Several herbs have cardiovascular benefits, such as lowering blood pressure, cholesterol levels, and triglycerides, which can contribute to a healthy heart and reduce the risk of heart disease.

8. Mood Enhancement

Some herbs have mood-enhancing properties that can help uplift mood, reduce anxiety, and promote mental clarity and focus, supporting overall emotional well-being.

9. Detoxification Support

Certain herbs aid in detoxification by supporting liver function, enhancing kidney health, and promoting the elimination of toxins and waste from the body, helping to purify and cleanse the system.

10. Weight Management

Many herbs can support weight management efforts by boosting metabolism, increasing satiety, and regulating appetite, making it easier to maintain a healthy weight and support fat loss goals.

Ten Herbal Supplements

Turmeric

Dosage: Start with 1/4 to 1/2 teaspoon per day, gradually increasing to 1-2 teaspoons if needed.

Usage: Add turmeric powder to soups, stews, curries, rice dishes, or smoothies. You can also mix it with warm milk or tea.

When to Use: Turmeric can be consumed throughout the day, but it's particularly beneficial when consumed with meals to aid digestion and promote overall wellness.

Garlic

Dosage: Use 1-2 cloves of fresh garlic per day, or equivalent amounts of garlic powder or supplements.

Usage: Add minced garlic to cooked dishes like pasta, stir-fries, roasted vegetables, or salad dressings.

When to Use: Garlic can be used in almost any savory meal. For maximum benefit, consume it raw or lightly cooked to preserve its active compounds.

Ginger

Dosage: Start with 1/4 to 1/2 teaspoon of ginger powder per day, or use fresh ginger equivalent. Adjust based on personal tolerance.

Usage: Incorporate grated or powdered ginger into smoothies, marinades, stir-fries, or hot tea. You can also use ginger paste in cooking.

When to Use: Ginger is excellent for digestion, so consume it with meals or before or after eating to alleviate digestive discomfort.

Rosemary

Dosage: There's no standard dosage for rosemary, but you can use 1-2 teaspoons of dried rosemary per day as a guideline.

Usage: Use dried rosemary to season roasted meats, potatoes, vegetables, or homemade bread. You can also infuse olive oil with rosemary for salad dressings.

When to Use: Use rosemary during cooking to impart its aromatic flavor and potential health benefits to your dishes.

Oregano

Dosage: Use 1-2 teaspoons of dried oregano per day, or as desired.

Usage: Sprinkle dried oregano over pizza, pasta sauces, grilled meats, or roasted vegetables. You can also use it in marinades or salad dressings.

When to Use: Oregano adds a savory note to Mediterranean and Italian dishes and can be used whenever these flavors are desired.

Basil

Dosage: Use 1-2 teaspoons of dried basil per day, or as needed.

Usage: Add dried basil to pasta sauces, soups, salads, or marinades. You can also use fresh basil leaves as a garnish or in sandwiches and wraps.

When to Use: Basil complements a wide range of dishes, particularly those with tomatoes, cheese, or Italian flavors.

Cinnamon

Dosage: Start with 1/2 to 1 teaspoon of cinnamon per day, or as recommended by a healthcare professional.

Usage: Sprinkle cinnamon over oatmeal, yogurt, fruit, or baked goods like muffins or pancakes. You can also add it to coffee, tea, or smoothies.

When to Use: Enjoy cinnamon with breakfast or as a flavor enhancer in sweet dishes and beverages throughout the day.

Thyme

Dosage: Use 1-2 teaspoons of dried thyme per day, or as desired.

Usage: Add dried thyme to roasted vegetables, poultry, fish, or soups. You can also infuse thyme in olive oil for salad dressings or dipping bread.

When to Use: Thyme pairs well with hearty, savory dishes and is commonly used in Mediterranean and French cuisine.

Sage

Dosage: Use 1-2 teaspoons of dried sage per day, or as needed.

Usage: Incorporate dried sage into stuffing, pasta dishes, soups, or sauces. You can also use fresh sage leaves as a garnish or in herbal teas.

When to Use: Sage adds a savory, slightly peppery flavor to dishes and is particularly popular in Thanksgiving stuffing and holiday recipes.

Parsley

Dosage: There's no specific dosage for parsley, but you can use a handful of fresh parsley leaves or 1-2 teaspoons of dried parsley per day.

Usage: Use fresh parsley as a garnish for savory dishes, salads, or soups. You can also add it to marinades, sauces, or homemade pesto.

When to Use: Parsley's fresh, bright flavor makes it a versatile addition to various dishes, providing color and a hint of freshness to your meals.

Learning Resources

This book has provided you with every detail that is necessary for a beginner to understand and get into the world of herbs and herbal remedies. But, if you want to learn more and explore everything more deeply, try the resources given underneath and enjoy the journey of herbal healing.

Books

"The Herbal Medicine-Maker's Handbook: A Home Manual" by James Green

"Rosemary Gladstar's Medicinal Herbs: A Beginner's Guide" by Rosemary Gladstar

"Medical Herbalism: The Science and Practice of Herbal Medicine" by David Hoffmann

"The Complete Herbal Handbook for the Dog and Cat" by Juliette de Bairacli Levy

"The Complete Illustrated Holistic Herbal: A Safe and Practical Guide to Making and Using Herbal Remedies" by David Hoffmann

Online Courses

Herbal Academy (https://theherbalacademy.com/)

The School of Natural Healing (https://www.snh.cc/)

Chestnut School of Herbal Medicine (https://chestnutherbs.com/)

Websites and Blogs

The Herbal Resource (https://www.herbal-supplement-resource.com/)

HerbMentor (https://www.herbmentor.com/)

The Herbal Academy Blog (https://theherbalacademy.com/herbalism-articles/)

Podcasts

The Holistic Herbalism Podcast (https://www.thepracticalherbalist.com/podcast/)

The Herbal Highway (https://kpfa.org/program/the-herbal-highway/)

YouTube Channels

Herbal Jedi (https://www.youtube.com/user/herbaljedi)

The Medicine Woman's Roots (https://www.youtube.com/user/SingingNettle)

The School of Evolutionary Herbalism (https://www.youtube.com/channel/UCZ7-OCDHBvRyJyQHVCWjG_Q)

Social Media Accounts

Herbal Academy on Instagram (https://www.instagram.com/herbalacademy/)

Rosemary Gladstar on Facebook (https://www.facebook.com/rosemary.gladstar)

Online Forums and Communities

Reddit's Herbalism Community (https://www.reddit.com/r/herbalism/)

HerbMentor Community (https://community.herbmentor.com/)

Herbal Conferences and Events

The International Herb Symposium (https://www.internationalherbsymposium.com/)

Online Herbal Databases

Plants for a Future Database (https://pfaf.org/)

The National Center for Complementary and Integrative Health (NCCIH) Herb Database (https://www.nccih.nih.gov/health/herbsataglance)

Herbalist Certification Programs

American Herbalists Guild (https://www.americanherbalistsguild.com/)

National Institute of Medical Herbalists (https://www.nimh.org.uk/)

Herbal Logbook

Herbal Log

Date:			Herb Name:		

Benefits/Applications:

Harvested	Planted	Yield	Diseases	Symptoms	Cures

Physical Appearance	Height	Care Instruction

Application and Dosage

Herb	Suitable Age Group	Dosage	Usage

HOW TO USE	TEA/TINCTURES	OIL/OINTMENT	ORALLY

Herbal Log

Date: | | Herb Name:

Benefits/Applications:

Harvested	Planted	Yield	Diseases	Symptoms	Cures

Physical Appearance | Height | Care Instruction

Application and Dosage

Herb	Suitable Age Group	Dosage	Usage

HOW TO USE	TEA/TINCTURES	OIL/OINTMENT	ORALLY

Herbal Log

Date:			Herb Name:		
Benefits/Applications:					
Harvested	Planted	Yield	Diseases	Symptoms	Cures
Physical Appearance		Height		Care Instruction	

Application and Dosage

Herb	Suitable Age Group	Dosage	Usage
HOW TO USE	TEA/TINCTURES	OIL/OINTMENT	ORALLY

Herbal Log

Date:		Herb Name:			

Benefits/Applications:

Harvested	Planted	Yield	Diseases	Symptoms	Cures

Physical Appearance	Height	Care Instruction

Application and Dosage

Herb	Suitable Age Group	Dosage	Usage

HOW TO USE	TEA/TINCTURES	OIL/OINTMENT	ORALLY

Herbal Log

Date:		Herb Name:			

Benefits/Applications:

Harvested	Planted	Yield	Diseases	Symptoms	Cures

Physical Appearance	Height	Care Instruction

Application and Dosage

Herb	Suitable Age Group	Dosage	Usage

HOW TO USE	TEA/TINCTURES	OIL/OINTMENT	ORALLY

Herbal Log

Date: Herb Name:

Benefits/Applications:

Harvested	Planted	Yield	Diseases	Symptoms	Cures

Physical Appearance	Height	Care Instruction

Application and Dosage

Herb	Suitable Age Group	Dosage	Usage

HOW TO USE	TEA/TINCTURES	OIL/OINTMENT	ORALLY

Herbal Log

Date:		Herb Name:			

Benefits/Applications:

Harvested	Planted	Yield	Diseases	Symptoms	Cures

Physical Appearance	Height	Care Instruction

Application and Dosage

Herb	Suitable Age Group	Dosage	Usage

HOW TO USE	TEA/TINCTURES	OIL/OINTMENT	ORALLY

Herbal Log

Date: | Herb Name:

Benefits/Applications:

Harvested	Planted	Yield	Diseases	Symptoms	Cures

Physical Appearance	Height	Care Instruction

Application and Dosage

Herb	Suitable Age Group	Dosage	Usage

HOW TO USE	TEA/TINCTURES	OIL/OINTMENT	ORALLY

Herbal Log

Date:			Herb Name:		

Benefits/Applications:

Harvested	Planted	Yield	Diseases	Symptoms	Cures

Physical Appearance	Height	Care Instruction

Application and Dosage

Herb	Suitable Age Group	Dosage	Usage

HOW TO USE	TEA/TINCTURES	OIL/OINTMENT	ORALLY

Herbal Log

Date: | Herb Name:

Benefits/Applications:

Harvested	Planted	Yield	Diseases	Symptoms	Cures

Physical Appearance | Height | Care Instruction

Application and Dosage

Herb	Suitable Age Group	Dosage	Usage

HOW TO USE	TEA/TINCTURES	OIL/OINTMENT	ORALLY

Herbal Log

Date:		Herb Name:			

Benefits/Applications:

Harvested	Planted	Yield	Diseases	Symptoms	Cures

Physical Appearance	Height	Care Instruction

Application and Dosage

Herb	Suitable Age Group	Dosage	Usage

HOW TO USE	TEA/TINCTURES	OIL/OINTMENT	ORALLY

Herbal Log

Date: | Herb Name:

Benefits/Applications:

Harvested	Planted	Yield	Diseases	Symptoms	Cures

Physical Appearance	Height	Care Instruction

Application and Dosage

Herb	Suitable Age Group	Dosage	Usage

HOW TO USE	TEA/TINCTURES	OIL/OINTMENT	ORALLY

Herbal Log

Date:		Herb Name:			

Benefits/Applications:

Harvested	Planted	Yield	Diseases	Symptoms	Cures

Physical Appearance	Height	Care Instruction

Application and Dosage

Herb	Suitable Age Group	Dosage	Usage

HOW TO USE	TEA/TINCTURES	OIL/OINTMENT	ORALLY

Herbal Log

Date: | Herb Name:

Benefits/Applications:

Harvested	Planted	Yield	Diseases	Symptoms	Cures

Physical Appearance	Height	Care Instruction

Application and Dosage

Herb	Suitable Age Group	Dosage	Usage

HOW TO USE	TEA/TINCTURES	OIL/OINTMENT	ORALLY

Herbal Log

Date:		Herb Name:			

Benefits/Applications:

Harvested	Planted	Yield	Diseases	Symptoms	Cures

Physical Appearance	Height	Care Instruction

Application and Dosage

Herb	Suitable Age Group	Dosage	Usage

HOW TO USE	TEA/TINCTURES	OIL/OINTMENT	ORALLY

Herbal Log

Date:				Herb Name:		

Benefits/Applications:

Harvested	Planted	Yield	Diseases	Symptoms	Cures

Physical Appearance	Height	Care Instruction

Application and Dosage

Herb	Suitable Age Group	Dosage	Usage

HOW TO USE	TEA/TINCTURES	OIL/OINTMENT	ORALLY

Herbal Log

Date:		Herb Name:			

Benefits/Applications:

Harvested	Planted	Yield	Diseases	Symptoms	Cures

Physical Appearance	Height	Care Instruction

Application and Dosage

Herb	Suitable Age Group	Dosage	Usage

HOW TO USE	TEA/TINCTURES	OIL/OINTMENT	ORALLY

Herbal Log

Date:			Herb Name:		

Benefits/Applications:

Harvested	Planted	Yield	Diseases	Symptoms	Cures

Physical Appearance	Height	Care Instruction

Application and Dosage

Herb	Suitable Age Group	Dosage	Usage

HOW TO USE	TEA/TINCTURES	OIL/OINTMENT	ORALLY

Herbal Log

Date:			Herb Name:		

Benefits/Applications:

Harvested	Planted	Yield	Diseases	Symptoms	Cures

Physical Appearance	Height	Care Instruction

Application and Dosage

Herb	Suitable Age Group	Dosage	Usage

HOW TO USE	TEA/TINCTURES	OIL/OINTMENT	ORALLY

Herbal Log

Date:			Herb Name:		

Benefits/Applications:

Harvested	Planted	Yield	Diseases	Symptoms	Cures

Physical Appearance	Height	Care Instruction

Application and Dosage

Herb	Suitable Age Group	Dosage	Usage

HOW TO USE	TEA/TINCTURES	OIL/OINTMENT	ORALLY

Herbal Log

Date:		Herb Name:			

Benefits/Applications:

Harvested	Planted	Yield	Diseases	Symptoms	Cures

Physical Appearance	Height	Care Instruction

Application and Dosage

Herb	Suitable Age Group	Dosage	Usage

HOW TO USE	TEA/TINCTURES	OIL/OINTMENT	ORALLY

Herbal Log

Date:		Herb Name:			

Benefits/Applications:

Harvested	Planted	Yield	Diseases	Symptoms	Cures

Physical Appearance	Height	Care Instruction

Application and Dosage

Herb	Suitable Age Group	Dosage	Usage

HOW TO USE	TEA/TINCTURES	OIL/OINTMENT	ORALLY

Herbal Log

Date:			Herb Name:		

Benefits/Applications:

Harvested	Planted	Yield	Diseases	Symptoms	Cures

Physical Appearance	Height	Care Instruction

Application and Dosage

Herb	Suitable Age Group	Dosage	Usage

HOW TO USE	TEA/TINCTURES	OIL/OINTMENT	ORALLY

Herbal Log

Date: | Herb Name:

Benefits/Applications:

Harvested	Planted	Yield	Diseases	Symptoms	Cures

Physical Appearance | Height | Care Instruction

Application and Dosage

Herb	Suitable Age Group	Dosage	Usage

HOW TO USE	TEA/TINCTURES	OIL/OINTMENT	ORALLY

Herbal Log

Date:		Herb Name:			

Benefits/Applications:

Harvested	Planted	Yield	Diseases	Symptoms	Cures

Physical Appearance	Height	Care Instruction

Application and Dosage

Herb	Suitable Age Group	Dosage	Usage

HOW TO USE	TEA/TINCTURES	OIL/OINTMENT	ORALLY

Herbal Log

Date:	Herb Name:

Benefits/Applications:

Harvested	Planted	Yield	Diseases	Symptoms	Cures

Physical Appearance	Height	Care Instruction

Application and Dosage

Herb	Suitable Age Group	Dosage	Usage

HOW TO USE	TEA/TINCTURES	OIL/OINTMENT	ORALLY

Herbal Log

Date:			Herb Name:		

Benefits/Applications:

Harvested	Planted	Yield	Diseases	Symptoms	Cures

Physical Appearance	Height	Care Instruction

Application and Dosage

Herb	Suitable Age Group	Dosage	Usage

HOW TO USE	TEA/TINCTURES	OIL/OINTMENT	ORALLY

Final Words

So, here we are, at the end of this herbal adventure together. It feels like we've shared a secret garden, full of whispering plants and promising remedies. I hope this book has been your trusty guide, leading you through the winding paths of herbal knowledge.

Remember, learning about herbs is like making new friends. Each plant has a story to tell, a gift to offer. You don't need to know everything at once. Start small, maybe with a herb you've always been curious about. Plant a seed, nurture it, and watch your herbal journey unfold.

I believe in the power of plants to heal and nourish. I've seen it firsthand in my own life, and I'm excited to share this passion with you. Whether you're whipping up a soothing tea or creating a healing salve, every step you take is a celebration of nature's pharmacy.

So, go ahead, experiment, and most importantly, enjoy the process! Your body, mind, and spirit will thank you. Happy healing

Printed in Great Britain
by Amazon

47474615R00123